D0868036

WORDS OF PRAISE FOR *BILLY*

Billy is a story of faith and the important role faith plays in making the right choices in life. It is also a love story—not only of Billy and Ruth Bell but of Billy's love for God and God's Word. It's the story of a young man who, by faith, accepted a call to preach, and lived his passion for proclaiming the Gospel of Jesus Christ.

—GiGi Graham, daughter of Billy and Ruth Bell Graham

Billy offers fresh insights into the life of a towering presence in American life, a man who for 60 years has figured prominently in annual Gallup surveys of the "Most Admired Men in the World." It is a solid historical account that speaks most like a novel with a continuous dialog that weaves the historical pieces together. The result is a book that beautifully captures the flavor of the times and the factors that shaped this remarkable servant of God.

—George Gallup, Jr., Former President of the
Gallup Organization (Gallup Poll), Founder
of the George H. Gallup Institute

Choices matter. They are the hinges on which swing the doors opening or closing for the rest of one's life. On Billy Graham's early choices swung a future that has deeply affected us personally and seekers around the world.

—Bill and Gloria Gaither, ASCAP's Gospel Songwriters
of the Century

Billy Graham is a national icon—an international treasure. This book is an inspiring read about how the foundations were laid in his life decisions to make him the man of God we all love and so deeply respect. A life well lived with incredible passion and integrity sets an example for each of us to reach for.

—Dave Ramsey, New York Times Bestseller,
National Radio Host

Billy is a thrilling account of how God orchestrated every event in Billy Graham's life to prepare and lead him to become His ambassador to the world. Despite his worldwide fame, Billy Graham has retained a servant's heart and has stayed true to his lifelong calling—to lead others to a personal relationship with God through Jesus Christ. His integrity and singleness of goal will motivate all who read this book to examine their own purpose in life. *Billy* is a guidebook for anyone who longs to experience an abundant, joyful, and purpose-filled life. It will inspire and encourage Christians and seekers alike.

—Denise Jackson, NY Times bestselling author of
It's All About Him and *The Road Home*.

Here is a good book about a good man! Read about Billy Graham, an inspiration for America and the world.

—George Foreman, World Heavyweight Boxing
Champion, Television personality, Entrepreneur

BILLY

THE UNTOLD STORY OF A YOUNG BILLY GRAHAM AND THE TEST OF FAITH THAT ALMOST CHANGED EVERYTHING

WILLIAM PAUL MCKAY

AND

KEN ABRAHAM

THOMAS NELSON

Since 1798

NASHVILLE   DALLAS   MEXICO CITY   RIO DE JANEIRO

© 2008 by Solex/MATP Venture

All rights reserved. No portion of this book may be reproduced, stored in a retrieval system, or transmitted in any form or by any means—electronic, mechanical, photocopy, recording, scanning, or other—except for brief quotations in critical reviews or articles, without the prior written permission of the publisher.

Published in Nashville, Tennessee, by Thomas Nelson. Thomas Nelson is a registered trademark of Thomas Nelson, Inc.

Thanks to Mark Sweeney & Associates, Bonita Springs, Florida 34135.

Page design by Mandi Cofer.

Thomas Nelson, Inc., titles may be purchased in bulk for educational, business, fund-raising, or sales promotional use. For information, please e-mail SpecialMarkets@ThomasNelson.com.

Note: This book is the unauthorized retelling of a true story and is based on actual events. Certain items have been adapted for dramatic effect, and some artistic license has been taken to assist in the flow of the storyline.

ISBN 978-0-7852-9832-8 (TP)

Library of Congress Cataloging-in-Publication Data

McKay, William Paul.
  Billy : the untold story of a young billy graham and the test of faith that almost changed everything / by William Paul McKay and Ken Abraham.
     p. cm.
  ISBN 978-0-8499-2067-7 (hardcover)
  1. Graham, Billy, 1918– 2. Evangelists—United States—Biography. 3. Templeton, Charles, 1915-2001—Friends and associates. I. Abraham, Ken. II. Title.
  BV3785.G69M29 2008
  269'.2092—dc22
  [B]

2008036002

Printed in the United States of America
10 11 12 13 14 LSI 6 5 4 3 2 1

To every seeker of truth who has ever dared to grapple with the great questions of life, and who has plunged into the vortex where faith and reason collide.

Acknowledgments

The only time I met Dr. Billy Graham was at a Hyatt Hotel in Century City, California. We were discussing the possibility of doing a documentary on his life. At the conclusion of the meeting, Dr. Graham turned to me and said, "My only concern is that my image on screen would eclipse the image of Jesus. I am at an age where I know that I will be standing before my Savior soon, and I don't want anything to disappoint Him." He went on to tell me that so many in the Christian world have elevated him to a level of which he did not feel worthy. As I left my meeting with Dr. Graham, I was struck by the awareness that he was one of the most humble men I had ever met. When Dr. Graham is gone from Earth, the true measure of the man will be more fully understood, and he will be profoundly missed.

As we endeavored to make the movie *Billy: The Early Years*, and write this book, I held Dr. Graham's two principles before me. Often I reflected on his words and realized that this standard was more important than the most optimistic commercial success for this project. For these reasons, we have worked hard to honor Billy Graham as a servant of Jesus Christ while not elevating him to a superficial sainthood. I sincerely hope we have met the standards Dr. Graham established and lived out over the past nine decades.

Additionally, I wish to thank Janet, my dear wife of thirty years. She was handpicked by the Father for my life. I cannot imagine a journey without the love of my life. Her laughter, love, and prayers have given me every gift I have needed.

My son, Grant, has been traveling and working with me for the past several years and has been indispensable at every turn in the making of the film and in the writing of this book. Thank you, Son; you are greatly trusted and loved.

Many people have stood in prayer to make this book and feature film possible. Some have gone far beyond anything we could have asked or expected, and without the prayers of these dear saints, you would not be holding this book. Special thanks to Cliff and Elvie Broderick; Jim, Julie, and Ashley Hilman; Mike and Mary Mugavero; Rand and Susanne McCullogh; Mike and Mary Hassett; Rachel Pisarek; Mrs. Roberta Hromas; Bonnie Sanders; Chet and Nell Holsipple, and Daryl Ward. You are loved, appreciated, and not taken for granted.

And finally, Tom Ivy. Tom Ivy was Dr. Graham's television director for many years. Tom's love and devotion for Dr. Graham became a part of the inspiration for this project.

As you turn the pages and read the words in this book, may the Lord be increased in your life.

William Paul McKay

The authors also express heartfelt thanks to Mark Sweeney of Mark Sweeney and Associates for believing in this project and expertly handling the many agent responsibilities associated with it.

Special thanks to Matt Baugher, Thomas Nelson Vice President and Publisher, who caught the vision for what this book could be, and to Jennifer McNeil, our managing editor, who helped facilitate this project each step of the way. Thanks to the great Thomas Nelson sales and marketing team as they take this never-before-told story to the world.

Chapter One

The gray hospital walls appeared unusually bland, a stark contrast to the elderly yet vibrant patient who occupied the lone bed in the private room. Outside, the chilly winter wind whipped against the room's window, frosting it over with a thin layer of ice, but the bright television lights and the press of busy people bustling around the patient threatened to raise the temperature inside significantly.

Charles Templeton, now in his early eighties, his physical and mental alacrity slipping away, had consented to be interviewed for a documentary film. A gifted author, popular Canadian TV broadcaster, successful sports columnist, consummate inventor, and former minister, Templeton ranked as one of the most intriguing characters of the twentieth century.

Once he was regarded as the world's greatest Christian evangelist, a close friend and role model to Billy Graham, packing in crowds of more than forty thousand people who came specifically to hear him speak. Now he was known as one of society's most outspoken atheists—though he preferred the term *agnostic*—having given in to his doubts about Christianity nearly fifty years earlier. He had encouraged Graham to do the same, but his friend had chosen a different path.

A kindly nurse fluffed Templeton's pillows behind him and respectfully prepared him for the cameras. She had already helped him shave and had attempted to comb his tangled gray hair into a style that at least appeared intentional. She then gently helped him push his arms into the sleeves of a burgundy robe that covered the top of his pajamas so he could look his best on camera. At eighty-three, Templeton was still remarkably handsome and charismatic, despite the debilitating effects of Alzheimer's disease. Though his body betrayed him more frequently these days, his voice remained a beautiful, mellifluous cross between John Huston and Walter Cronkite. No one at the hospital ever doubted that the person who possessed that voice had once stood before throngs of people, mesmerizing them with his eloquence and keen intellect.

Ever distinguished—*dashing* and *debonair* were aptly applied terms in his younger days—and meticulous about his appearance, Templeton exuded a sophistication and class that belied his blue-collar upbringing and lack of formal education. He had abandoned public school following completion of the ninth grade and hadn't returned until age thirty-three, when he was granted special admission to Princeton University—well after he had established a successful career. He rarely misspoke but instead prided himself on wooing with his words the admiration of the nurses more effectively than many a young suitor could have done, even with flowers, candy, or expensive gifts. Yet as quickly as Charles Templeton could turn on the charm, there were still brief moments when the cautious, well-rehearsed person seemed to disappear, revealing the frettings and mumblings of a deeply tormented soul.

"That light's too hot," the cameraman cautioned as he and a gaffer repositioned their equipment in the tight hospital room.

"This light?" the gaffer asked, pointing at a large photography light directly above Templeton's head.

Templeton didn't notice the light, the camera, or the young men in his room. Instead, he seemed obsessed and somewhat agitated. "Get away . . . get away . . ." he mumbled, looking wildly around the room as if following some invisible ghost.

"Sir?" the gaffer asked politely as he turned toward Templeton. "Is there anything I can do for you?"

The old man recovered quickly, shook his head slightly, and looked at the camera operator and gaffer as though they had just entered the room. "It's good to see you again, young man. I thought yesterday's interview was very productive."

The gaffer glanced toward the cameraman, who simply shrugged his shoulders. The gaffer turned back toward Templeton. "I'm pretty sure we'll be out of your hair by the end of the day," he said, pulling the overhead light a few inches away from Templeton's face as he spoke.

"That's too bad," Templeton replied. He gazed intently at the men preparing the room for the interview. "I'll miss you. I'll miss all of you."

Deborah Matthews, an attractive though heavily made-up woman in her mid-fifties, paced anxiously on the other side of the room, talking on a cell phone, her back to Templeton. Matthews knew this was her chance, maybe her last chance, to get back in the flow of things at the network. For the past ten years or more, she had received fewer and fewer features as the producers increasingly leaned toward younger, slimmer reporters. The powers that be wanted more than fresh news; they wanted fresh faces, skin without wrinkles, eyes that still retained the sparkle of youthfulness. And more than anything, they wanted controversy, something with some sizzle and pizzazz. This wasn't just the news business anymore; it was entertainment dollars they were after, and if one news organization could not or would not provide the scandal and innuendo that audiences craved, another would soon replace it in the ratings.

Deborah Matthews had been relegated to second-rate stories for so long now that she had almost forgotten what sizzle felt like. But she still recognized a great story when she saw one, and this Templeton guy had an angle like no one she had ever interviewed. Nevertheless, after nearly two full days of shooting, she had produced about as much excitement as an obituary. Now her boss, Bradley Benjamin Post, was on the phone, wanting to know why.

"I can't get a rise out of him," she whispered into the cell phone. "You were wrong—there's no dirt here about Graham. And if there is, we're not going to get it out of this Templeton guy. He's a professional charmer and—"

"Cut the nonsense, Deborah!" Post bellowed into the phone, so loudly that the sound man in Templeton's room heard him, glanced up from his control panel, and looked at Deborah quizzically. Deborah held the cell phone at arm's length, away from her ear, as though expecting another blast. The sound man nodded in understanding.

In New York, the quintessential "get me the story," chain-smoking, coffee-chugging TV news producer was rapidly losing patience with his former star reporter. "Look, Deborah," Post said hotly, "I've been protecting you for the past six months. You know that the network is reducing its workforce, and your job is on the line. The young girls are coming up—and they're hot—so if you don't get the dirt on Graham, I'll find someone else who will."

"But, Brad, it's not there!" Deborah protested. "Even Templeton himself says there's no scandal—no misuse of funds, no sexual dalliances, no lavish lifestyles—"

"Don't tell me it's not there, Deborah!" Post fumed. "It's got to be there! These evangelists are all alike. They can't keep their fingers out of the till or their hands off the adoring female fans. I know there's scandal in Graham's life somewhere. Templeton knows it too, and your job, Deborah, is to find it. Find it, or find yourself a new occupation."

Deborah Matthews turned pale as the ramifications of Post's words hit her full force. She knew he was right about the aggressive young reporters. They were no longer nipping at her heels; they were tugging at her stockings. She knew, too, that Bradley Benjamin Post cared almost as little about loyalty to his staff as he did about the truth. What did he care that Deborah had been with the network longer than most of the debutante reporters had been alive? What did it matter whether or not any dirt Templeton might dish was true? All that mattered to Bradley Benjamin Post were ratings—ratings that Deborah had not been able to pull since the advent of cable news, with its bevy of brainless beauties doling out prepackaged ditties read straight off the teleprompters.

Deborah knew what Post expected; she was aware of the rules of the game. If there was no scandal to be found, at least give the impression that there might be. Slant the story, shape the questions, or tweak the lead lines in such a way as to imply something shocking to the public. Take some minor point out of context and bore into it; milk it; color it; make it into something with . . . yes, with *sizzle*; and then keep throwing it out, louder, bolder, more frequently, until what started as a half-truth at best grew into a bold-faced lie. Soon, with the aid of the right camera angle and creative editing, that original, innocuous point could somehow be morphed into the "previously untold *truth*."

Deborah had been counting on Templeton as her hot ticket back to the big time, and frankly, so had Post. That's why he had given her the assignment. They had been friends and colleagues for years, but Deborah knew she had to pull this story out on her own. Brad had gone to bat for her in New York one too many times, and although she had scored outstanding scoops and earned numerous accolades in her illustrious career, those days were long past. She understood that much, yet she had underestimated Post's desperate desire to do what no other television or print medium had been able to do—successfully pin some scandal on Christianity's most Teflon hero, Billy Graham.

"Whatever you have to do, Deborah, do it! No one has ever before approached this story from this angle. Push every button; don't hold anything back," Post said quietly but emphatically. "I know Templeton has never betrayed his old friend Billy Graham, but there has to be some animosity in there somewhere, some-thing you can use to pit them against each other. Templeton was the hottest preacher in the world till Graham came along. Even *after* Graham came along. But something happened. Find out, Deborah. Squeeze something out of the old man before he kicks the bucket. Why did Graham ascend to the top of the field, and why did he and Templeton part ways? There has to be more to this story than has been told. Find it, Deborah," Post implored, then added under his breath, "or else."

In her peripheral vision, Deborah caught a glimpse of Templeton waving his arms in the air, again at nothing. The reporter shifted her body slightly in his direction just as the man in the hospital bed cried, "Get away . . . get away from me!"

She grimaced and raised her eyebrows. "Talk later, Brad," she said abruptly as she flipped her cell phone shut. Deborah turned toward the gaffer. "Slate it, Dave."

"But the light—"

"I said slate it, Dave. Now!" the reporter snapped.

The gaffer rolled his eyes and exhaled a puff of air. He picked up a documentary slate and held it toward the camera lens.

"Speed . . . rolling," the cameraman said.

The gaffer spoke louder than necessary, as though trying to make a point. "'Faith Lost' documentary. Charles Templeton interview, tape three." He slapped the slate together and stepped to the side, allowing the camera to focus on Templeton and the ambitious reporter.

Deborah Matthews was already in Templeton's face, leaning toward him like a gambling addict staring longingly at a roulette wheel. "You said, 'Get away,'" she said. "Who do you want to 'get away'?"

Templeton responded as though he had not even heard her question, which, perhaps, he had not. "I like talking to you. Must you finish the interview today?"

Ms. Ambition hedged, not wanting to drag out the interview longer than necessary, but unwilling to miss any morsel Templeton might drop. "We may be back tomorrow," she replied.

Templeton fussed with his collar. "That would be marvelous."

"Is there anything—anything at all—that you'd like to tell us about your . . . er, shall we say, 'friendship' with Billy Graham?"

The old man's eyes lit up. He nodded his head and spoke quietly but with deep emotion. "Billy Graham . . ."

"Yes, Billy Graham," the reporter pressed. "Did you ever feel angry or jealous that Billy—"

"Billy was such a fine young man," Templeton said as much to himself as to the reporter. He seemed to be viewing his own mental motion picture as he spoke. "A farm boy, really. That's where we were, wasn't it, when we left off yesterday? We were talking about when he worked on the farm?"

"Yes, Mr. Templeton, and that is all quite interesting," Matthews said dismissively, "but I would love to hear more about *your* relationship with Billy. I've read some of your books and have heard some of your comments about Christianity and evangelists. I know that you two experienced some tension in your relationship. Tell me about that."

Templeton waved his hand in small circles. "All in due time, dear lady. All in good time. You must have patience. I will tell you everything—things you've never before heard about Billy and me—but this information is crucial to understanding who Billy was—and, of course, who I was, and who we had become by the time our paths crossed."

"Yes, sir, I understand that, but—"

"In due time." Templeton's voice rose in volume as he nodded. "You will not be disappointed, I assure you. Now, where were we?"

Deborah exhaled emphatically. "Whatever comes to mind," she said, making no attempt to conceal her exasperation. "Tell us how you feel about Billy."

Templeton's facial expression slipped into a quasi-smile. He had seen her kind before. He'd spent years dealing with reporters; he knew what they wanted, what they needed. "You want something"—he loved the word—"*juicy*, don't you?"

"No, I just . . ."

Templeton smiled openly now. He waved his hand again as if swatting at a persistent mosquito. "I told you before. There's no scandal there," he said straightforwardly. "No embezzlement. Billy was . . ."

Deborah's head snapped up from her notes, her eyes riveted on Templeton's. "Yes. What was he really?"

Templeton seemed to almost sigh as he said softly, "Billy . . . was a sweet, good man. He just *believes*. End of story."

Deborah scowled but remained undaunted. She was close to a scoop. She could feel it. "All right. Let's go back. What about you? You were the star, not Graham."

"Me?" Templeton shrugged, and a hint of a smile crossed his face. "Well, you are correct, young lady. Before I was consumed with intellectual doubt, self-criticism, and an unending search for personal truth, I was a much better preacher than Billy. Much better! Just ask him." Templeton's eyes twinkled in the bright light. "He's an honest man. He'll tell you."

"Then how did a farm boy become more popular than you? How did a fellow who was not as smart as you, not as articulate as you, and . . ." Matthews paused and cocked her head coyly, "I might add, not nearly as handsome as you . . . how did he become the famous evangelist Billy Graham?"

Templeton's voice increased in volume. "Billy Graham!"

"Yes, sir. I've researched your life and his too. I know you used to be close friends. I've read about the two of you preaching in America and in Europe together. I know how those two prostitutes in Paris tried to seduce you and Graham when you were both virile young men."

Templeton smiled again. "That could have happened yesterday, young lady. Prostitutes? Who said anything about prostitutes? They were fine, wholesome young women . . . much like yourself."

"Ahem," Deborah cleared her throat and shifted uncomfortably in her chair. "Yes, do you really think Billy ran away from that naked woman?"

Templeton leaned forward in his bed, suddenly energized. "Billy Graham? I thought you wanted to talk about me. I'm the one who's dying. I'm the one who is soon going to need the epitaph. His story is dull! Mine is the story you should tell. Billy? There's nothing juicy there. Okay, give him a medal for being a Boy Scout, but that's all. Dull. Dull as butter."

"If that's the case, why does everyone know who Billy Graham is, but no one knows who Charles—"

"I'll tell you the truth: *I don't get it,*" Templeton interrupted, sitting up straighter. "No, sir. I don't get it. Any intelligent man, any person with half a brain at all looking around at the world today would have to come to the conclusion that there could not possibly be a loving God."

Clearly agitated, Templeton shook his head slowly from side to side as though lamenting the loss of a loved one. "But not Billy," he said. "Billy believed. He took the lesser road of faith, rather than the more vigorous endeavor of intellectual pursuits." He nodded in self-agreement, then cleared his throat and said loudly, "And he committed intellectual suicide."

"Really?" Deborah Matthews was intrigued.

Backing away from Deborah's baited question, Templeton softened his tone. "Look, I'm not saying he's a phony. Far from it. He's the genuine article. He actually believes all that stuff he preaches. I disagree with him profoundly on his view of Christianity and think that much of what he says in the pulpit is puerile nonsense. But there is no feigning in him. He believes what he believes with an invincible innocence. He is the only mass evangelist I would trust."[1]

Templeton was watching the mental movie again, transporting himself back in time. "Billy was my friend," he said wistfully. "My best friend, really. And I daresay that I was his—at least I was for quite a season . . .

"We were both products of the Depression. My mother raised six children all alone after . . . after my father deserted her. We rented out rooms to strangers; our kidneys ached because there was only one bathroom. In the wintertime, I used to sift through the furnace ashes searching for any unconsumed nuggets of coal. I scoured the neighborhood looking for broken branches or pieces of discarded wood, anything that would burn and give us a little warmth during the freezing Canadian winter. There were days when we had no food at all, no sustenance, not a morsel. And we crouched in the darkness, frozen like frightened animals, until the bill collector left our door."

Templeton took a deep breath. "In contrast, Billy's life was like a . . . I'll tell you what it was . . . It was like a fairy tale."

"A fairy tale?"

"Yes, Billy Graham came into this world in 1918, little more than a year after Lenin's Bolshevik revolution in Russia." Templeton rubbed his chin and chuckled. "Who'd have thought that he and I would live long enough to see freedom returned to the Russian people?"

Deborah nodded as Templeton continued. "Billy and I grew up during the Roaring Twenties. I lived in Canada in those days. He lived in a wood-frame farmhouse outside Charlotte, North Carolina,

---

1. Charles Templeton, *An Anecdotal Memoir* (Toronto: McClelland & Stewart Limited, 1983), 74.

and he grew up in a Norman Rockwell painting. His family wasn't rich, but they sure weren't poor; they had a dairy farm, after all. Although the bottom had dropped out of the economy due to the Depression, the Graham family had loyal customers who still needed milk, even when there was little money with which to buy it."

Templeton paused, as though he were watching the years roll by on a screen in front of his eyes. "Our story—Billy's and mine—it is quite ironic, when one stops to think about it. We were both born and raised during interesting times; both were poor students." Templeton let out a slight laugh. "Billy did worse in school than I did, you know, but at least he graduated from high school and college. And we were both athletes in our younger years. I was much better than him, of course."

"Of course," Deborah repeated.

"We both became preachers, almost against our wills, and we were two good-looking fellas who knew how to stir up the crowds."

"Yes, tell me more about that."

"Oh, you can't start there," Templeton said. "You Americans, always in a hurry. You get upset if you miss a spot in a revolving door."

It was Deborah's turn to sigh. "Okay, you tell me, Mr. Templeton. Where does the story start?"

"On a farm, of course," Templeton replied. "Billy worked hard on the farm, along with his parents and siblings, but somehow, he always found time for baseball.

"Believe it or not, in the spring of 1934, all Billy ever wanted to do with his life . . ." The old man in the hospital bed halted again, as though he recognized that the story he was about to tell was so outlandish that he might not be believed. "All Billy wanted to do was to play *baseball*!"

Chapter Two

CHARLOTTE, NORTH CAROLINA, SPRING 1934

"Way to go, Billy!" called a farmer wearing a pair of bib overalls covering a faded plaid shirt.

"That's my man, Billy," added Albert, an African American farmhand who worked on the Graham property. Albert looked at the farmer and grinned. The farmer raised his arms above his head, clasped his hands together, and shook them like a victorious boxer. Albert's chocolate-colored face glistened in the sunshine, his smile radiating joy at Billy's triumph. "You're the boss man, Billy!" he called out.

Driving his uncle's yellow convertible, with the radio blaring, Billy Frank Graham and several other players, still dressed in their dirty baseball uniforms, were waving to the people along the street, singing along with the music on the radio and relishing their victory as they slowly paraded through downtown Charlotte. Several fawning girls were in the backseat, and three others sat atop it where the convertible top was buttoned down, the girls reveling along with the players.

From the driver's seat, Billy spotted Albert in the crowd along the sidewalk. "Hey, Albert!" he called out and waved.

Albert waved back at Billy, then turned to the farmer standing next to him. "See? Billy's the man!" he said proudly.

In the car ahead of Billy was sixteen-year-old Grady Wilson, one of Billy's best friends. Grady's car, like Billy's, was decked out with jubilant baseball players and pretty girls all waving and singing along to the music on the radio. As the impromptu parade spun its way through the streets, with horns honking and radios blaring, shop owners and other bystanders came outside to cheer and greet the victorious baseball players. Bleary-eyed from the Depression, Charlotte's impoverished working class looked for any reason to find hope, and a group of overly enthusiastic baseball players provided just the sort of lift to the town's spirits that they sorely needed.

Easing the yellow convertible past the Charlotte Cinema, Billy looked up at the old theater's marquee and read, "*Little Women.*" The tall, thin, wavy-haired Billy Frank Graham didn't have a lot of extra money to go to the movies, but he had all the "little women" he could handle right there in the car, along with his friend Thomas Walter Wilson, Grady's older brother, whom everyone simply called T. W. for short. Billy really liked girls; he was "in love" with a different one almost every week, it seemed. And the girls genuinely liked Billy as well, with his lanky frame; his upbeat, outgoing personality; his congenial smile; and his bright, piercing blue eyes.

A familiar song came on the radio, and as T. W. waved to the crowd, Billy sang along loudly, although horribly off-key. T. W. winced at the sound, then looked over at Billy and slapped him on the back. "I knew you were onto that fastball, Billy!"

Billy just smiled and adjusted the rearview mirror to get a better look at two of the pretty girls perched on the backseat of his car. He sure hoped they had heard T. W.'s compliment.

The girls whispered to each other and then giggled. Billy was just about to return his gaze to Grady's car in front of him, when the two girls suddenly leaned forward and kissed Billy simultaneously, one on each side of his face, leaving bright-red lipstick marks on both of his cheeks. T. W. and the other fellows in the car howled in laughter. Billy laughed too, and his faced flushed almost as red as the girls' lipstick.

Feigning hurt feelings, T. W. twisted his body around toward the girls. "Hey, what about me?" he pleaded. "A bunt's gotta count for somethin'."

The girls playfully shoved him back down in his seat.

"Nothin'?" T. W. chortled. "That's what I get for my bunt—nothin' at all!"

It was late afternoon by the time Billy returned his uncle's convertible and rode his bicycle back to the Graham dairy farm. He hastily shed his dusty baseball duds and hopped into the bathtub. The hot water felt soothing as he closed his eyes, soaked, and relaxed in the tub for a few minutes, his long arms dangling limply over the edges of the creamy-white porcelain. He could have easily fallen asleep right there, but he knew his mother would have dinner ready soon. He washed quickly, toweled off, and put on a crisp, clean shirt and a fresh pair of overalls, held up by suspenders. He rolled up his sleeves and hurried out to the barn to get a few chores done before dinner. There was never a lack of work to be done on the Graham farm, with more than four hundred acres to care for and at least seventy-five cows to be milked and attended to morning and evening. Yet Frank Graham didn't mind his son

Billy's obsession with baseball—as long as he got his chores done each day.

It was still light outside, but the sun was nearly setting by the time Billy got back to the house and entered the screened-in porch where the family liked to eat dinner on warm evenings. Walking in, he saw his mother, Morrow Graham, and the children—Jean, age four; Melvin, ten; and Catherine, thirteen—setting the table. Albert, the hired hand, was there too. He had been with the Grahams so long that he seemed like family, and the Grahams treated him that way.

Reaching for a bouquet of freshly picked flowers already displayed on the table, Billy snatched them and held them behind his back, away from his mother's view. Morrow Graham bustled back and forth between the kitchen and the porch, the dinner table taking shape more and more with each trip. Placing a large bowl of mashed potatoes on the table, she looked up at Billy, standing nearby.

"Mmm, since when did you start wearin' lipstick?" she asked with just a hint of a smile and a twinkle in her eyes.

"What? Oh . . ." Billy's hand flew instinctively to his cheek, landing right at the spot where one of the pretty girls had kissed him. Embarrassed, and wondering how he could have missed the lipstick during his bath, Billy wiped his cheeks on the shoulder of his shirt. Straightening up, his six-foot, two-inch frame tall and erect, Billy awkwardly reached out his arm and handed his mother the freshly picked bouquet of flowers.

If Morrow recognized them, she gave no such indication. Instead, she simply smiled, graciously received the bouquet from Billy, and drew him to her in a warm embrace. While Morrow loved all her children, she shared a special bond with her son Billy Frank.

"Where's Dad?" Billy asked when his mother released him and continued setting the table. Morrow gestured toward the field out back behind the farmhouse.

Billy stepped over to the screen and peered into the yard. Frank Graham, Billy's father, and a group of five other farmers were gathered near the house, standing in a circle around a large, old tree stump. Frank had changed from his work clothes and now wore a brown vest and necktie. Some of the men were dressed in their bib overalls; others looked as though they were ready for church. All had serious expressions on their faces. Billy recognized the men as part of a Christian Men's Club, formed after famed evangelist Billy Sunday conducted services in Charlotte a decade earlier. The club's membership had waned in the years since but had recently become more active, perhaps due to the many business failures, personal bankruptcies, and other dire circumstances brought on the community by the stock market crash of 1929 and the subsequent Great Depression. In May 1934, about thirty members of the group had met on the Graham property for an entire day of fasting and prayer. The men gathered outside while the wives met in the Graham home to pray for Charlotte's economic renewal and, more important, spiritual revival. Today's group of six was an offshoot of that original assembly.

Even from a distance, Billy could tell that they were not discussing the baseball game. He strained his ears to hear what his father was saying.

Frank Graham possessed the grave demeanor and personality of a rugged, hardworking man of the earth. His gravel-toned voice sounded sonorous and serious as he spoke. "For some time, we have been gathering around this ole tree stump, asking God for one thing," he said. "We have been believers for one thing."

Each man acknowledged Frank's words with nods of affirmation.

Frank continued, "*By faith*, we are going to put God to the test. On this day in Charlotte, we are going to ask God to give this nation—no, *all* nations—a voice to preach the gospel to the ends of the earth. Are we all agreed on this one thing?"

The men's faith seemed to expand almost palpably, taking hold of each one of them as they prayed. Frank reached out his hand to the man on his left and then on his right. Awkwardly at first, the men clasped hands, and then one by one, each of the others joined hands in strong, solid agreement.

The men's prayer echoed that of Vernon Patterson, a member of the original thirty who had met at the farm, who had prayed aloud, "Oh Lord, out of this very city, out of Charlotte itself, may You raise up such a one as will go out and preach Your gospel to the ends of the earth." Patterson's prayer had no doubt been oft repeated by all of the men during the discouraging postdepression days.

Billy pressed his nose against the porch screen, barely able to hear his father's plaintive plea. "God, You know us as men of the soil. We have touched Your earth with our hands, and You have given us, each of us, great harvests in these difficult times. But now . . ."

Catherine placed a pitcher of sweetened ice tea on the dinner table and then stepped up to the screen and stood next to Billy. "Look at that, Billy," she said with reverential awe.

"Well, '*look at that*' is right," Billy responded cynically. "I guess somebody sweet-talked Daddy into usin' our property—"

Morrow Graham had been arranging plates on the table, her back to Billy and Catherine, but when she heard Billy's caustic remark, she turned around quickly to confront her son. "Billy Frank, your daddy has some very personal reasons for the way he feels. Maybe someday he'll share them with you. Until then, I expect you to be respectful, young man. Do you understand me?"

Surprised by his mother's reaction, Billy looked at his dad, then back to his mother. "Yes, Momma," he said contritely.

Religiosity did not come naturally to fifteen-year-old Billy, who loved pulling pranks as much as any boy his age. Even at the Presbyterian church in Charlotte, where his family attended services when he was a boy, Billy had a difficult time paying attention to Dr. W. B. Lindsay, the monotone pastor who preached clad in a formal black ministerial robe. While parishioners fanned themselves in the hot sanctuary, Billy sat several rows behind the family pew with his friends T. W. and Grady. Rather than praying, singing, or listening to sermons, the boys often spent their time in church working feverishly on several well-crafted spitballs.

One Sunday morning, sitting a few rows in front of the boys was a quintessential, stuffy church lady with her hair arranged in a large, exquisitely constructed bun atop her head—the perfect target. When paper and saliva were formed just right, Billy let the first missile fly. Bull's-eye! The spitball disappeared somewhere in the mound of hair. Billy prepared to launch again, while Grady and T. W. pretended to cough, barely able to contain their laughter. Again, a perfect shot! This time, however, the mountain of hair moved as the woman slowly turned around and glared at Billy and his friends. Struggling to maintain their composure, the boys sat up straight and nodded in agreement with whatever Dr. Lindsay was saying. They didn't dare look at one another. One twitch of the lips and they would all convulse in gleeful laughter.

From the pulpit, Dr. Lindsay noticed the disturbance, and for a brief moment his eyes connected with Billy's. Billy quickly diverted his own gaze and stared toward the front of the pulpit. A few seats ahead, Morrow Graham noticed the object of the pastor's attention. Instantly she turned around and gave Billy "the look." Billy knew what that meant. It was time to straighten up, or Sunday dinner at the Graham household would not be a pleasant experience for anyone—least of all, him!

On most days, however, mealtime at the Graham farmhouse was a special gathering time for the entire family. Although Frank and Morrow Graham lost their life savings when the bank failed in 1933, they always had food on the table, thanks to hard work and the productivity of the dairy farm. Sometimes the pickings were a little slim, but Morrow always made the food stretch.

One night in late August 1934, the family was seated around the table, waiting for Frank Graham to offer a prayer of thanks. While the others stared hungrily at the steaming hot serving bowls filled with fresh corn, dinner rolls, beef, and mashed potatoes, Frank waited patiently for Billy, who was fascinated by a flyer announcing the upcoming revival services to be conducted by evangelist Dr. Mordecai Ham. The flyer and a local newspaper bearing an offensive headline about the preacher lay open on a small table behind Billy's chair.

Frank had waited long enough. He bowed his head, and the rest of the family followed suit. Frank began to pray slowly and emphatically, "For what we are about to receive, Lord, make us truly grateful." Billy bowed his head and closed his eyes. He didn't mean to be disrespectful, but he knew there was no rush. Frank Graham had been known to pray so long the food got cold. Billy was thankful that tonight's dinner prayer was one of his father's shorter ones. "In the name of our Savior and Lord, Jesus Christ, amen," Frank concluded.

"Amen!" Billy said loudly.

"Amen," Morrow agreed softly.

"Pass the sweet tea, will ya, Billy?" Frank asked.

Billy picked up the large, five-quart jug of tea and passed it to his father. The family members dug in without hesitation, passing food, hungrily filling their plates and eating. Billy, however, was still intrigued by the Mordecai Ham announcements.

"What's this doin' here?" He waved the paper and flyer so everyone could see them.

Frank had a mouthful of food, but he abruptly stopped chewing and stared at Billy, never taking his eyes off his son. Billy railed, "Don't tell me . . ." Billy turned to look at his mother. Morrow gave her head a slight shake, as if to say, *Don't go down that road, Billy Frank Graham.*

Too late; Billy was already wound up. "It's just that . . . I heard this travelin' preacher is just like all the others, a fleecer of the flock."

Morrow cringed at her son's cynical remark. "Billy," she said quietly.

"I'm just sayin', this is all Charlotte needs—another money-grabbing Elmer Gantry." An avid reader, though mostly of non-fiction, Billy was acutely aware of the Sinclair Lewis novel in which a preacher became a womanizer and a crook who bilked his audiences of their hard-earned money. Although a work of fiction, the novel had forever fixed the image of traveling evangelists as profiteering preachers at best and oftentimes little more than outright hucksters.

Nevertheless, the Christian Men's Club had invited Mordecai Ham to Charlotte—Ham, who described himself as a "hog-jowl and turnip-green" preacher, the kind of minister Abe Lincoln might have enjoyed, a man who, when he preached, "looked like he was swatting flies."

Like most people who had been praying for their city, Frank Graham regarded Ham's upcoming services—planned to run from August till after Thanksgiving—as an answer to prayer. Austere, cool, and distant, Frank could be a man of few words—and his few words were about to be spoken.

"God listens to everyone, Billy," he said firmly, "money or no."

"But I'm just sayin'—"

"You sure have a lot to say."

Billy attempted to make his point, but his father wasn't willing to hear it. "Well, I'm just sayin'—," Billy began again before Frank cut him off.

"I hear what you're sayin', son. Now, eat."

An awkward silence suddenly enveloped the room as Billy and his mother exchanged looks.

Catherine whispered to Billy, "I like Dr. Ham, Billy."

Albert nodded toward the two oldest Graham children. "I like him too," he whispered.

Under his breath, and trying to avoid having his father hear him, Billy muttered, "You may like him, but I'm just sayin', two things I'll never be: a preacher or an undertaker!"

Frank put his fork down, clanging it more loudly than necessary against his plate. "Son, how do you come by all of what you're 'just sayin'?"

"Well, everyone at school has been sayin', 'If you've seen one evangelist, you've seen 'em all,'" Billy replied gingerly.

A kind, good-hearted man, if a bit brusque, Frank Graham wanted to be fair to Billy, but he was not about to accept such disrespectful thinking. "You heard from a bunch of people who don't know," he said. "Maybe you ought to hear for yourself. If not, you're just repeating somebody else's ignorance. Ignorance, boy. I don't wanna hear 'nother word. Understand?"

Billy and Frank exchanged a tense look. "Yes, sir," Billy said quietly. Frank turned his gaze toward his plate and concentrated on his food. The conversation had left a bad taste in his mouth. Billy looked over at his mother, and her eyes communicated a combination of compassion, sorrow, and disappointment to him. She had always taught Billy to question, not to accept everything at face value, and her husband's attitude seemed a bit too dogmatic for her liking.

The Mordecai Ham meetings had been going on for several weeks before Billy and Albert decided to visit and make up their own minds about the vaunted evangelist. People were coming each evening from miles around to attend the services conducted in a temporary outdoor "tabernacle." Billy parked the Graham pickup in one of the few spots still available in the field. A corny version of the song "I'll Fly Away" was on the truck radio, so Billy turned the dial to another station—and soon a black gospel song pulsated through the static. Billy fiddled with the radio dial until the song came in perfectly. Then he turned up the volume, looked over at Albert, and smiled. For a few minutes, they sat in the truck, listening to the song and watching the throng of people streaming toward the tabernacle. People of all ages—mostly white, but some "coloreds" too—crowded into the parking lots in their cars, on horses, and a few even on donkeys.

As Billy and Albert took in the sights, suddenly Billy saw a familiar face. It was T. W. Wilson on his way to the tabernacle. Billy called out to T. W., but his voice was drowned out by the robust, enthusiastic singing that was coming from inside the tent.

Albert looked over at Billy and said, "Are we gonna sit here an' listen to the radio or go inside and see us a revival?"

Billy turned off the truck's engine and hopped out. "I can't believe I'm doin' this," he said to himself more than to Albert, as they closed the doors and headed toward the tabernacle.

Dressed in a blue suit that was too big for him and wearing a white shirt and tie, Billy followed Albert to the tent. Awkwardly, almost timidly, Billy entered the tabernacle. "Catch ya on the other side, Albert," he said, waving, then cringed as he watched Albert leave him and head toward the back left corner of the tent—the "colored" section. Segregation bothered Billy, but this was the South in 1934, and it would be another thirty years before Billy and others like him would help bring segregation to an end in Charlotte.

The service had already started, and the turnout was significant, so empty seats were difficult to find. But there, right down front, was T. W. Wilson, and it looked as though another person could squeeze in next to him on the end of the row. Billy made his way to the front of the tabernacle, not at all happy that the sawdust on the ground made his freshly shined shoes dirty all over again. T. W. saw Billy coming and slid over, making room for him on the end of the row. "Thanks, T. W.," Billy said as he slipped in beside his friend.

With the music playing and the audience singing a rousing gospel song, Billy took time to get his bearings, furtively glancing around the tabernacle and attempting to take it all in without making it too obvious that he was a newcomer. On the platform, a small choir, in which his sister Catherine was singing, helped lead the audience, although many of the people in the tabernacle seemed to know the old camp meeting–style songs by heart. Billy had never been all that interested in spiritual things, especially emotion-laden revivalist activities, so he felt more than a little out of place, especially sitting so near the action. As his eyes wandered, he leaned over and whispered to T. W., "I see the men getting ready to fleece the flock back there." Billy gestured to the ushers standing at the back of the tent, holding some buckets in which they would collect the evening's "freewill offering."

T. W. ignored Billy's remark. "Enjoy the moment, Billy," he said. "You'll never see nothin' like this again."

As the final song subsided, Dr. Mordecai Ham rose slowly and strode to the pulpit, obviously confident in his abilities. Dr. Ham was everything that Billy had heard of and more. A portly man, with thinning hair and an even thinner moustache that looked as though it had been penciled on his face, Mordecai Ham fit the prototypical image of the "fire and brimstone"–style preacher. Loud, bombastic, and not above stepping out from behind the pulpit and down from the platform to stand face-to-face with his audience, Ham preached hard. Oftentimes he peppered his messages with "you" rather than "we," pointing his finger in front of a man or woman's face as he brandished the Bible and castigated the crowd for their sins, causing his listeners to feel that he was speaking directly to each of them individually rather than corporately.

Billy wasn't accustomed to such straightforward preaching; Dr. Lindsay would never risk offending someone by confronting sin so overtly. Yet despite Dr. Ham's abrasive approach, Billy couldn't take his eyes off of him. Every word seemed to sear straight into his heart, mind, and conscience. Just as he tried to pull his thoughts away from the preacher's message, Dr. Ham hammered home another point. Billy shook his head slightly, trying to regain his composure. Dr. Ham was laying a strong foundation.

"As I have traveled all throughout the South and have seen up close the full effects of this Great Depression on our land," the preacher said in a quieter, calmer voice, "I can understand why some of you, maybe all of you, want to 'fly away' some glad morning."

A murmur, mixed with a few somewhat hesitant amens, rustled through the crowd.

Dr. Ham continued, his voice rising slightly as he spoke. "Well, I have some important news for you tonight. News that you might not find so welcome. News that's going to make you stop and think." The preacher paused and looked around at his listeners.

"Preach it, brother," someone called out.

"Tell us the truth. Don't hold back," another person encouraged.

Dr. Ham didn't need much encouragement. He knew precisely where he was going with his message. His voice more emotional now, he declared, "You cannot work your way to heaven!"

"No!" a voice responded near the front of the crowd.

"You cannot beg your way into heaven!" Ham's voice was louder now, more emphatic.

"That's right!" someone in the back of the audience called out.

"You cannot buy your way into heaven!"

"No, sir! That's for sure."

"You cannot bribe your way into heaven!"

The response from the crowd was immediate. "No!"

Ham could have driven home his point at any time now, but he continued drawing the audience down the sawdust trail. "You cannot climb your way into heaven!"

The number of people preaching back to the preacher grew even larger. "No!" they cried out.

Like a professional fisherman, confident of a large catch, Dr. Ham began casting out his net. "Your best efforts are filthy rags in the presence of almighty God. None of us is all good. Not a single one. We are each imperfect. We are each wanting in the eyes of the Lord. Sinners. Each and every one!"

A graying, well-dressed man stood up and waved the newspaper containing the offensive headline about Dr. Ham. "Who do you think you are?" he shouted, to the shock of the audience. "Coming to our town and smearing the good name of our citizens?"

Ham fearlessly bounded down from the platform and strode straight down the aisle toward the dissenter. He snatched the newspaper from the man's hands and held it up for all to see. "Who am I?" he boomed. "I am Dr. Mordecai Fowler Ham." Ham handed the newspaper back to the heckler, wheeled around on his heel, walked back to the platform, and hopped back onto the stage. "And God has told me that there is sin in this town. And He told me where. I am the messenger. And now I have a question to ask of you: I ask the young men right there. Yes, you!" Suddenly the famous evangelist was pointing his long finger right at T. W. and Billy.

The boys exchanged surprised glances. Then Ham pointed more specifically, directly at Billy. "What brings you here, son? Your own two feet? No!" Ham answered his own rhetorical question, and Billy was glad that he had done so, since he doubted his ability to form intelligible words at that moment.

It didn't matter. Ham knew the answer, and he wanted the congregation to understand it too. "Two thousand years before you were born, God planned for you to be here tonight," he seemed to say directly to Billy. Ham stretched out both of his arms in Billy's direction, his hand and fingertips forming a shape similar to a six-shooter. "You think this is an accident? Well, let me tell you, young man. You feel an emptiness in your life. And you can't fill it with a fancy car or a pretty girl. It's there, gnawing at you, and you can't fill it. You say to yourself, 'How do I get into heaven? I'm just an

average man. Sometimes I'm good. Sometimes I'm bad. Sometimes
I've got love blooming in my heart, and sometimes it's dark as the
devil! Sometimes I know where I'm going, and sometimes I am
lonely and lost.'"

The crowd murmured in agreement, but Billy was perplexed.
He felt as though Mordecai Ham was speaking only to him. T. W.
sat spellbound, hanging on Ham's every word as though com-
pelled to listen.

Ham bore down hard on his listeners now. "You will die in
your sin unless you do something about it!"

Audience members responded to Ham's forthright message
in different ways—some were affronted, some shamed, some
convicted.

Ham didn't mind. He was pulling in the nets. "And guess
what? You are not alone."

Billy leaned closer; his heart was beating faster; he was almost
afraid to listen to anything more that the preacher had to say—yet
he didn't want to miss a word.

"And this is the good news. Our Lord Jesus Christ cares for
each and every one of you."

The preacher pointed to the man with the newspaper, who
was still standing as though awaiting his opportunity to refute the
evangelist's words.

Dr. Ham continued, "He loves you. Even you. Yes, you; I'm
talking to you, son. Jesus will never leave you nor forsake you."

The audience seemed to offer a collective sigh. "Amen!"

Ham grew friendlier in tone. "Why did Jesus volunteer to die
for us?"

"Tell us!" someone in the audience called out.

Dr. Ham smiled slightly before continuing. "Tonight, Jesus

offers you forgiveness and purpose for your life. If you want to free your soul of heartache, of doubt, of anxiety, of pain, come! Come down here to the front, and let's pray."

The choir began singing quietly as people all over the tabernacle shot from their seats and streamed down the sawdust-covered aisle. Billy watched in awe as Albert became one of the first to walk forward, mixing right in with the white people at the front who were confessing their sins and asking God to forgive them.

"Come down. Come show the Lord Jesus Christ your total commitment," Billy heard Ham say through the din. "Come down! Make a physical statement for Christ by walking down this well-worn, sawdust trail. You're not alone. Come! Come now, while there is still time . . ." Ham didn't explain what he meant by "while there is still time," but whether he was speaking of time left in the evening's service, time before God's judgment, or time remaining in each person's life, his words took effect.

The song leader stood up and began leading the congregation in the hymn "Just as I Am," singing all four verses. Billy watched, astounded to see that the man who had been waving the newspaper now dropped it on the sawdust and went forward, a repentant look on his face.

People crowded to the front, some standing, others kneeling, some even sitting on the ground. Many were weeping, confessing sins they had committed against God and one another.

As more and more people made their way to the front of the tabernacle, Billy watched with skeptical interest at first, his cynicism turning slowly to amazement as he saw people he recognized responding to Mordecai Ham's invitation. A woman near Billy began weeping, then stepped out and walked down the sawdust aisle. These people weren't off-center kooks. Some of them were highly intelligent; some were "uptown," sophisticated folks; and some were just common, everyday people, like Billy himself. The more Billy watched, the more enraptured he felt.

As the choir began to sing the thought-provoking old revival invitation hymn "Almost Persuaded," Billy, almost to his own surprise, stood to his feet. Hesitating just a moment, he conquered his reticence. Then, with head held high, he made up his mind. The moment he took one step, he was no longer almost persuaded; he was fully committed. He walked determinedly to the front of the tabernacle to pray with the others. As he looked up at the platform, he saw Catherine in the choir. Suddenly the other singers seemed to disappear, and it was just Catherine singing to Billy—to nobody else in the entire world but him alone. The choir was again singing "Just as I Am," and Catherine's sweet, pure voice rang out: "Just as I am, without one plea, but that Thy blood was shed for me . . ." That refrain permeated Billy's heart and mind, and it seemed to echo over and over again deep within him.

It was a song that Billy Graham would hear many times in his lifetime.

Late that evening, after Billy and Albert returned to the Graham dairy farm, Billy sat outside on the front bumper of the pickup for a long time, pondering what he had experienced at the meeting. What had he actually done by stepping out "in faith," as the preacher had said, and walking to the front of the tabernacle? He had prayed, just as the "counselor" who had come alongside him had recommended, and he had asked Jesus Christ to come into his life, but he didn't feel any different. And yet he believed that some sort of genuine commitment had been made between himself and God that night. What did it all mean? he wondered.

Albert came by on his way from the barn. He looked at Billy and for a long moment considered whether it might be helpful to talk about what they had seen, heard, and encountered firsthand, but then Albert thought better of his idea. Let Billy bring it up when he was good and ready. "'Night, Billy." He raised his hand nonchalantly as he spoke.

"'Night, Albert," Billy replied, still lost in thought.

Before Billy drifted off to sleep that night, he knelt beside his bed and prayed a simple but deeply meaningful prayer. "Oh, God, I don't understand all of this," he said, "but as best as I can figure out, I've given myself to You."

Chapter Three

CHARLOTTE, 1934

Morning found Billy and Albert carrying pails of milk, freshly drawn from the herd of cows they had directed one by one into the milking stalls. With more than seventy cows to be milked, it was no easy chore. Most of the milk went into large metal milk cans, some of which held thirty to fifty gallons. The cans were tightly sealed to preserve the freshness, then stored in the icehouse till they could be transported or sold to local customers. Some of the daily production, of course, was used by the family itself.

Billy wiped the perspiration from his brow and put down his pails of pure-white milk near the large tree stump out in the backyard. Just as he did, his mother walked up behind him, nearly taking him by surprise. "'Mornin', son. 'Mornin', Albert," she said with a musical lilt in her voice.

"'Mornin', ma'am," Albert answered respectfully.

"Good morning, Momma," Billy responded.

"You must have been out pretty late last night," Morrow said. "Was it a long team meeting?" Morrow Graham knew her son well, and she knew that a more direct probe into the events of Billy's evening might cause him to be reluctant to talk about it. Like most mothers, she knew already where her son had been before she asked. In fact, she and her husband, Frank, had been in the same place, and they had watched with grateful hearts as Billy walked the aisle.

"I didn't go to the team meeting," Billy said, his blue eyes practically begging his mother to question him further.

"Oh? Where were you then?"

Billy and Albert exchanged knowing looks.

"Um, I'll just get these pails of milk up to the house," Albert said, grasping the pail handles and heading for the farmhouse.

Billy looked at his mother, who didn't say a word. She didn't have to. Her eyes asked the question: *Well?*

Billy swallowed hard. "I went to the tent revival."

Morrow feigned a surprised expression, not upset, merely intrigued. "Oh, I see." Then she smiled and started walking slowly toward the house, but when Billy touched her arm gently, she stopped and turned to him.

"Momma, did you . . . did you talk to Dr. Ham about me?"

"Did I what?"

"You know, did you tell him anything about me? That preacher, Dr. Ham. He said all these things about me in front of everybody else."

"Things?" Morrow's interest was piqued. "Mmm, things. No, I never talked to that preacher, Billy Frank. Not one word."

Frank Graham popped his head out of the barn, and when he saw Billy's canister of milk on the ground, he called out, "Billy, get that milk up to the icebox, boy."

"Yes, sir," he called back, then bent down to grab one of the pails. But suddenly, looking back at his mother, he stopped short. Reaching inside his overalls' pocket, he pulled out a crumpled Bob Jones College brochure that someone had given him at the meeting. Billy smoothed the brochure and handed it to his mom. "I got this at the tent revival," he said.

Morrow gazed at the brochure, taken aback, yet pleased at the same time. She knew that Billy had been leaning toward attending the University of North Carolina, so the brochure describing an education with a biblical worldview pleasantly surprised her. She took it all in, and then in a soft voice she said, "Billy Frank, don't be afraid to ask questions. Don't ever be afraid to question."

Billy wasn't completely sure what his mother was implying, but he understood that her words were fraught with more meaning than she was willing to say. Looking at the strong woman he admired so much, he simply answered, "Yes, ma'am."

ᏹ

TEMPLETON'S HOSPITAL ROOM, 2001

Charles Templeton nodded his head and placed his arms across his chest, nearly brushing against the microphone clipped to the collar of his sweater. "And what followed from that?" he asked, looking at Deborah Matthews but obviously not expecting her to reply. "Nothing," he groused. "A decision to preach the gospel? No! He wanted to be a baseball player! If he had been scouted, that's what he would have done, too. But the truth is, he was a rather lackluster athlete. An above-average-sized fish in an extraordinarily small athletic pond."

Templeton paused and smiled as he recalled how Billy often boasted of his brief stint as a semipro baseball player. A fairly good athlete himself in his younger years, Templeton never truly believed that Billy had anything other than normal athletic prowess. His smile broadened as he thought of how he had teased Billy at a summer conference in Canada when, during a pickup softball game, the tall, gangling Graham had approached the plate, grasping his bat cross-handed.

Then, just as quickly, Templeton's smile disappeared, his expression indicating that he had stumbled on to something truly important. "Would you like to know what my religious conversion was like?" he asked, leaning forward slightly. "While Billy was squeezing udders down on the farm . . ."

☙

Toronto, 1930s

By his own admission, Charles Templeton had no interest in religion during the first nineteen years of his life. His interests lay in sports and in drawing. One Sunday afternoon when Chuck was only twelve, he drew a sketch of Felix the Cat, a popular comic strip character. With eyes longing for acceptance and approval, young Templeton took the drawing to his father, William Loftus Templeton, who had retired to the parlor with a batch of reading materials and a package of figs, purposely closing the French doors so as not to be disturbed by the family members.

But on this particular day, a precocious adolescent did brashly interrupt his father's solitude by holding out the sketch of Felix the Cat for him to see. Loftus Templeton looked up from his reading and noticed the drawing. "Very good, Chuck," he said. "Was it done freehand?"

"Yes," the boy answered, not quite sure how his father might respond.

"You have a talent for drawing," the man said as he passed the sketch back to his son and returned to his reading. "Keep it up."

His father's praise wasn't exactly gushing, but it was enough to spur on the younger Templeton. Although he was a poor student in school—he failed ninth and tenth grades before transferring to Toronto's Western Technical School to study art—his love for drawing continued to grow, as did his skill. While still in art school, Chuck combined his interest in sports and his passion for drawing to create three sketches of some Toronto Maple Leafs's hockey players. He then took them to the sports editor of one of Toronto's leading newspapers, and as a seventeen-year-old art student, he was hired to work as a sports sketch artist in the midst of the Depression.

Chuck's drawing skill endeared him to the Toronto sports community, and before long, his sketches were syndicated to eighteen newspapers in Canada. Best of all, he was being well paid. Life in the raunchy world of the sports newsroom, however, offered its own "rewards," and soon young Templeton discovered its temptations.

His father—the handsome son of a Methodist minister—had abandoned the family when Chuck was fourteen. With Toronto, as well as the rest of the world, in the throes of the Depression, Chuck's mother scrambled to keep food on the table, eventually turning their home into a boardinghouse to make ends meet.

Five years later, Chuck's mother underwent "a religious experience," as Templeton later somewhat caustically referred to it, although he acknowledged that her newfound faith changed her entire outlook on life. "She looked better, sang as she went about her housework, and seemed filled with an inner happiness."[1] She soon influenced the others in the family too, and they all—all except Chuck, that is—attended together the Church of the Nazarene, a denomination similar to old-time Methodists. While Chuck appreciated his mother's sincerity and was happy for the renewed vim her religion provided her, he still wanted nothing to do with religion. Indeed, his mother's piety made him downright uncomfortable. He much preferred having a few beers with the boys from the sports bureau to having Communion with the banal believers at the church.

Then one night in 1936, after attending a party overflowing with crass jokes, obscene laughter, and too much drinking, Templeton returned home around 3:00 a.m., feeling unusually depressed. When he passed the mirror at the entrance of his mother's home, he saw himself in the glass, and as he later put it, "I didn't like the man I saw there."[2]

He tried to sneak past his mother's bedroom, but she heard him and called out to him. He went in and sat on the side of her bed, listening only halfheartedly as she talked to him about God and the joy her faith had brought her, and how she longed to see Chuck in church along with her other children. As she spoke, Templeton took inventory of his sordid, wasted, empty life. When

---

1. Charles Templeton, *An Anecdotal Memoir* (Toronto: McClelland & Stewart Limited, 1983), 327.

2. Ibid, 336. Note: Some researchers have concluded that the date of Templeton's conversion was more likely 1934, since he was nineteen years of age at the time; but in his book, he set the date at 1936, although it is possible that Alzheimer's had already somewhat blurred his memory.

he could take no more, he wished his mother good night and went to his room.

But a darkness pervaded his heart and mind. He later described what he was feeling: "It was as though a black blanket had been draped over me. A sense of enormous guilt descended and invaded every part of me. I was unclean."[3]

Ↄ⊂

TEMPLETON'S HOSPITAL ROOM, 2001

Deborah Matthews had long since stopped looking at her notes and was instead sitting mesmerized by Templeton's tale. She could scarcely imagine one of the world's most noted agnostics having the type of experience the aged Templeton was describing.

"I began to pray," Templeton related. "My face upturned to the heavens, tears streaming, and the only words I could find were, 'Lord, come down. Come down. Come down' . . .

"And in a moment, a weight began to lift—a weight as heavy as I. It passed through my thighs, my belly, my chest, my arms, my shoulders, and lifted off entirely. I felt I could have leapt over a wall. An ineffable warmth began to suffuse every corpuscle. It seemed that a light turned on in my chest, and its refining fire cleansed me. I hardly dared breathe, fearing that I might end or alter the moment. Somewhere in that darkness I heard a still, small voice, mine own, whispering softly over and over, 'Thank you, Lord! Thank you, Lord, thank you . . . thank you . . . thank you.'"[4]

---

3. Templeton, *An Anecdotal Memoir*, 34.

4. Ibid.

Charles Templeton, the man some called an atheist or at best an avowed agnostic of more than forty years, paused dramatically, looked straight into the camera, and roared, "That, by Christ, is a conversion!"

Chapter Four

TORONTO, 1936

While Charles Templeton later came to renounce his faith, he never disparaged his conversion experience. He rationalized it on the basis of his yearning for a father figure in his life or a sense of obligation to repay his mother for her years of loneliness. He even, in an attempt at self-analysis, suggested that his acceptance of his mother's faith could have been a response to the guilt he felt over his adolescent sexual experiences. But despite his efforts to explain his "born again" experience, he never denied that something of deep significance had transpired that night in his bedroom. After all, how could he? The very same night of his profound encounter, he returned to his mother's bedroom. One look at his face, and she said, "Oh, Chuck!" and knew immediately that something dramatic had occurred in his heart. She burst into tears of joy; then after regaining her composure, she talked with Chuck till almost dawn.

When Chuck finally went back to his own room, the morning

sun was already climbing above the eastern horizon. He slipped into bed and lay there motionless, basking in new life, "bathed," as he put it, "in a radiant, overwhelming happiness. Outside, the birds began their first tentative singing, and I began to laugh, softly, out of an indescribable sense of well-being at the center of an exultant, all-encompassing joy."[1]

When Templeton took his faith to work, he quickly discovered that his brand of religion was frowned upon and mocked. He became the butt of raunchy jokes and not-so-subtle innuendos. Before long, Templeton told his boss that he was leaving the Toronto newspaper to go into the ministry.

"Good luck, Chuck," his boss told him. "I think you're nuts, but good luck."

While Chuck Templeton was coming to terms with his newfound faith and enduring the off-color jokes of his sports department colleagues, young Billy Graham was working as a Fuller Brush sales representative, hoping to earn enough money to pay his way through Bible college.

∾

TEMPLETON'S HOSPITAL ROOM, 2001

Charles Templeton leaned back and closed his eyes momentarily. Deborah Matthews, his tenacious interviewer, feared he had fallen asleep right in the middle of the conversation. But then, suddenly, Templeton's head snapped up as he said, "Did I mention that Billy . . ."

---

1. Templeton, *An Anecdotal Memoir*, 34.

"Yes? What about Billy?"

Templeton's body seemed to relax—in commensurate contrast to that of the intense reporter—at the thought of Billy Graham going door-to-door, trying to convince penniless housewives that they needed an expensive hairbrush or cleaning utensil. Templeton smiled slightly. "Billy could really sell those Fuller brushes. The summer before he went off to college, he became quite the door-to-door salesman."

"Wonderful," Deborah said flatly.

Of course, what the reporter didn't realize was that Billy Graham's experience as a Fuller Brush salesman was tremendous training for the future world's greatest evangelist.

&

NORTH CAROLINA, SUMMER 1936

The Fuller Brush Company was founded in 1906 by twenty-one-year-old Nova Scotia entrepreneur Alfred C. Fuller. Determined to make the best products of their kind, Fuller's product credo was simple: "Make it work; make it last; guarantee it no matter what." He went door-to-door selling custom-made hairbrushes out of a suitcase. As he recruited others to do the same, his company became well-known as an opportunity for an ambitious, personable individual to earn a good profit. And if young Billy Graham was anything, he was ambitious and personable. He and his friends Grady and T. W. Wilson signed on with Fuller for the summer.

Despite dire predictions by his father and uncle that he'd be a failure as a salesman, Billy put on his best outfit, grabbed his suitcase full of samples, and hit the road, traveling all over North and South Carolina, peddling his wares.

Wearing a sports jacket, tie, and a traditional men's fedora, his start was a bit shaky. He knocked on the door of a potential customer, then stepped back and practiced his memorized sales spiel as he waited for someone to answer. When a housewife tentatively opened the door, holding it slightly ajar, Billy flashed a big smile and nervously launched into his sales talk.

"Hello, ma'am. My name is Billy Graham, and I am here to change your . . . um . . . ahh, er . . . to change your life."

Recognizing the innocuousness of her caller, and somewhat amused at his audacity, the housewife said, "And tell me, just how are you going to do that, Mr. Billy Graham?"

Encouraged, Billy fumbled for his brush samples. "Well, I have here . . ." He opened his suitcase full of sample brushes and accidentally dumped them all over the porch.

The housewife smiled, feeling remorseful about causing the young man to drop his wares. She felt rather sorry for the bumbling brush salesman.

Billy's face turned a deep shade of red. "Oh, excuse me, ma'am," he said nervously, dropping to his knees and gathering his brushes into a pile in the center of the suitcase. He stood up, smiled again, attempted to regain his composure, then started his prepared speech from the beginning.

"I am going to show you the finest brush Fuller has to offer," he said, holding up one of his samples. "No, it's not this one," he said, reaching for another brush and holding it up in front of the bemused housewife. "Actually, it's not this one." He fumbled around in the suitcase, looking for another brush. Billy continued to work his way through nearly every brush in the suitcase before he found the prized brush.

"Ah, here it is. The favorite of every woman in the county. Well, no, let me say, it is the favorite in the entire state of—"

"How much do I owe you?" the kindly woman asked.

Billy looked at the woman, then at the brush he was holding, the disorganized mess of brushes in the suitcase, then back to the woman. "Really?"

"Yes, really," the woman said with a smile. "Give me your best brush."

"Yes, ma'am!" Billy quickly pulled out his note pad and began writing out the details of the housewife's order. He didn't want to give her time to change her mind.

Following his first sale, Billy's confidence soared. At the next home, he rapped at the door and could hardly wait till someone opened it. When an unwitting woman opened the door, an extremely confident Billy Graham, successful Fuller Brush salesman, was ready for her. He unobtrusively slipped his foot next to the door to prevent the home owner from closing it before he could launch into his spiel. "Hello, ma'am. My name is Billy Graham, and I am here to change your life!"

As the summer progressed, so did Billy's sales skills. Contrary to his father's predictions, he proved to be a natural salesman. His sincerity, enthusiasm, and vibrant yet gracious personality disarmed even the most unwilling potential customer. He sold as many or more brushes simply on the merits of his personality as he did by pointing out the features of the brushes in his sample case. Convincing someone of his or her need for what Billy had to offer was good training for his future career, although Billy saw it at the time simply as a means to earn some money for school.

The experience as a traveling salesman prepared Billy in some other ways as well. It was his first venture away from home for any prolonged period of time, and for the most part, he was on his own. Scrimping and saving every penny, Billy sometimes found himself staying in some rather rough and unsavory hotels or boardinghouses, where the clientele were not always as kind, sober, or moral as the folks back home. It was Billy's first insight into the realities of life for many people who had not grown up in the safety or security of a loving family.

⁊

TEMPLETON'S HOSPITAL ROOM, 2001

Deborah Matthews frowned with displeasure and raised a hand in Templeton's direction, causing him to pause in his story. "Mr. Templeton, that is all well and good," she said disingenuously, "but it sounds to me like you sincerely admired Billy. And yet you later spoke harshly to him and publicly castigated the man and his ministry. Why, you practically proclaimed him an idiot for believing as he does."

"I never called him an idiot," Templeton said matter-of-factly. "Other things, perhaps, but never an idiot. I always respected Billy as a person; it was our beliefs that drove a wedge between us, as you shall soon see."

Templeton smiled impishly at the reporter. He seemed to relish the image of himself as a brilliant intellectual and Billy as a brush salesman almost as much as he had the picture of Billy as a mediocre baseball player. He would have preferred to linger on those subjects longer, but he could tell that the reporter and her crew were growing impatient in their search for more tantalizing morsels. He pursed his lips, knowing that he had no scandalous revelations to offer, but he didn't care. He was enjoying immensely the memories playing in the theater of his mind.

"Thus, since he wasn't going to be a baseball player," Templeton said, raising his index finger provocatively, "young Billy went to a little Bible school. Bob Jones College. Not even an accredited school yet." Templeton shook his head slightly in mock disgust. "The most constipated learning environment of its time. Not to mention a social nightmare. Men, keep your distance from the women; and may the two sexes never meet! The Gospel according to Bob Jones. Deviate one iota to the left or right, and you faced the wrath of Dr. Bob Jones himself!"

Certain now that Templeton was about to reveal a titillating tidbit, Deborah Matthews leaned forward eagerly.

❡

BOB JONES COLLEGE, CLEVELAND, TENNESSEE, 1936

Bob Jones College was originally founded in Florida by its namesake in 1927, but in 1933 Jones moved the school to Cleveland, Tennessee. It remained there until 1947, when the school moved to Greenville, South Carolina, where it exists today. An extremely conservative fundamentalist Christian, Jones established an institution of higher learning based on Christian values, but run much like a military base. The school had rules and regulations for everything, it seemed to young Billy Graham, including a demerit system for inappropriate behavior such as being late for class, loitering in the hallways, or talking to a member of the opposite sex without a proper chaperone. For a winsome farm boy who enjoyed kissing all the girls he went out with, Bob Jones College soon proved too restrictive for Billy, even though he truly desired to learn more about the Bible and how to apply its teachings to daily life. The school posted prohibitive signs at various places on campus. For instance, on Billy's dormitory wall was a sign warning, "Griping not tolerated." Worst of all, it seemed to Billy that the legalism fostered by the college filtered down from the top, stifling creative thought and discouraging any questioning of the biblical teachings as they were presented.

Billy never forgot his mother's admonition, however, to ask questions. His questions were not always well received at BJC, but Billy kept right on asking, especially when he had the opportunity to discuss doctrine with the big man himself.

"What are we discussing here today?" Dr. Bob asked Billy as he leaned back in his large leather office chair at the far end of a conference room–type table.

Billy stood at the opposite end of the table. "Well, sir, I have a lot of questions, and . . ."

"Ask away," Jones interrupted. "Don't be shy."

Billy looked at the college founder and took a deep breath. "Sir, it's a question about . . . asking questions, I guess." Dr. Bob nodded, not necessarily approvingly, but Billy took the nod as an affirmation. He opened the floodgates and let the issue flow out. "The other day in evangelism class, I asked the teacher a question about your philosophy and Calvinism. Just to get clear on it. But the class allows for no debate. Maybe I'm not getting something here, but how do we learn without thinking things through and asking questions?"

Billy was on a roll, but Dr. Jones cut him off short again. "That's the beauty of how we teach at Bob Jones College, son. I've answered all the questions; I've made all the mistakes. There just aren't any more to be made. I've made them all for you. And that is my gift to you and all my students."

Billy wasn't convinced. "I just don't understand academic studies that permit only one man's interpretation of doctrine and Scripture," he said.

Dr. Bob would hear none of that. He stood to his feet and peered menacingly at Billy. "You don't understand?"

"No, sir. I'm just a little unclear about—"

"Well, let me clear things up for you. This place is called Bob Jones College. Not Billy Graham College." Dr. Bob's face looked flushed as he spoke.

"I have tremendous respect for you, sir. But I'm not sure I fit in here. I'm not criticizing, just asking. Just searching for ideas and answers. It was the way I was raised. I was taught to think for myself. My momma—"

"Your momma!" Dr. Bob was irate now. "*God* gave me this position—not your momma! And I am doing His work in the way He has shown me to do it. Do you wish to defy the hand of God?" The way Jones couched the question, it was clear that there was only one correct answer.

Billy chose another. "No, sir. Maybe just yours."

"Young man, you will never, never, never amount to anything!" Jones railed. "Do you hear me, son? What I see ahead for you is nothing but failure. Failure, failure, failure, and *more* failure!"

Chapter Five

Charles Templeton, even advanced in years, still had an accurate perception of the clout someone such as Dr. Bob Jones had in the mid-to-late 1930s Christian community. He attempted to enlighten his jaded interviewer on the subject, it being obvious that somebody like Deborah Matthews could not possibly relate to the risk Billy Graham was taking in bucking Jones's influence.

"In those days a character like Dr. Bob was second only to God Himself," Templeton explained. "You did not say boo to one of those old-time preachers."

The reporter nodded in pseudo-understanding, hoping that Templeton would soon get onto something juicy and totally missing the point that Templeton was trying to make.

"But Billy stood up to him with respect and demanded intellectual freedom. And if he couldn't get it at Bob Jones College, he'd search for it somewhere else."

ℰℐ

FLORIDA BIBLE INSTITUTE, 1937

Indeed he did. Shortly after Billy went home for Christmas break, he and his family visited relatives near Tampa, Florida. While there, they stopped by the campus of Florida Bible Institute, a small but beautiful institution, equally committed to teaching biblical truth but not nearly as regimented as Bob Jones. A former country club that had gone under due to the Depression, in addition to its students and faculty, the Institute welcomed visiting preachers and Christian leaders who vacationed there. Many of the students enjoyed interacting with these great ministerial heroes, pumping them for their stories, and learning vicariously through their experiences.

Billy enrolled in early February 1937, but not before Dr. Bob warned him one last time, "Billy, if you leave and throw your life away at a little country Bible school, the chances are you'll never be heard of. At best, all you could amount to would be a poor Baptist preacher somewhere out in the sticks."[1]

Dr. Bob may have been many things, but his record as a predictive prophet proved to be quite lackluster.

It took courage for Billy to walk away from Bob Jones College, but he did it—luring one of his best friends, T. W., along with him to Florida Bible Institute. As the two young men drove toward Florida, with the car radio blaring, Billy's sense of freedom seemed to expand with each mile they traveled down the road. Finally they

---

1. William Martin, *A Prophet with Honor* (New York: Harper Perennial, 1992), 70.

arrived at the idyllic campus located in Temple Terrace, about twelve miles northeast of Tampa, set at the end of a long lane of mature trees covered in Spanish moss.

At the initial gathering of the faculty and student body that Billy and T. W. attended, the president and academic dean of the school, Rev. John Minder, a sympathetic, red-haired, gentle man, addressed the assembly from behind the podium. In addition to his duties as dean, Minder was also the pastor of a thriving congregation, Tampa Gospel Tabernacle, a church he had founded. In stark contrast to Dr. Bob Jones, Dean Minder exuded a mild spirit combined with a passion for learning.

"You will find that the basis of our teaching here at Florida Bible Institute," said Dr. Minder, "comes from our belief in the inspiration and authority of the Word of God."

Seated beside T. W., Billy let out a huge sigh of relief. Realizing that his was a lone response, Billy anxiously looked around the small, relaxed gathering. Much to his surprise, nobody had even noticed his almost giddy pleasure that the Bible, rather than someone's interpretation of it, would be his main textbook.

"Our staff is here to help you inquire, question, and learn to *think for yourselves*," Dr. Minder continued. "We are here to guide you and to assist you in this at times difficult but deeply satisfying journey . . ."

Billy and T. W. exchanged a glance. Billy knew they had come to the right place.

That impression was further confirmed as Billy plunged into his studies at Florida Bible Institute.

One afternoon, as the spring sunshine flooded through the windows of the classroom, Dr. Minder wrote the word *Evangelist* on the chalkboard.

"The term *evangelist* is from the Greek word meaning 'one who announces good news,'" he explained. "And what is the good news? Simply this: that Jesus Christ died to pay the penalty for our sins and to reconcile us to God. He rose from the dead and now reigns as Lord, offering forgiveness of sins and the liberating gift of His Spirit to all who repent and believe."

Dr. Minder walked slowly around the classroom, looking into the faces of his students as he spoke. "Some of you may be called to be pastors, others will be teachers, and some will be evangelists. Spiritual leaders do not all have the same gifts or callings. While they all may handle some of the same material from the Bible, their roles are different. The pastor is to care for the people, shepherding the flock, you might say. The teacher is to explain the Word of God—to expound upon its meaning, to educate in how to apply the Word to every situation in any facet of society—and the evangelist is to primarily communicate the core message of the gospel. While the pastor and teacher may explain all sorts of doctrine and deep theological truths, or apply biblical principles to various walks of life, the evangelist is essentially concerned with one thing: presenting the good news, and hopefully presenting it in such a way that men, women, and children will decide to follow Christ."

Listening intently, Billy was intrigued; he wanted to hear more, but the chapel bell sounded, signaling the end of class. The students rose immediately, some interacting about what Dr. Minder had been saying, others engaging in the usual after-class banter. As Billy gathered his books and started for the door, he nearly bumped into Emily Cavanaugh, a beautiful, dark-haired young woman. For an awkward moment, both Billy and Emily stood still, staring face-to-face. Finally, Billy managed a smile, and Emily returned his smile with one of her own.

"Um, howdy," Billy blurted clumsily.

"Hi," Emily replied, her eyes locked onto his. Neither of them noticed that Dr. Minder was still giving last-minute instructions to the class.

"Don't forget to sign up for our outreach program. Lots of opportunities for budding preachers."

Dr. Minder's words caught Billy by surprise. He knew nothing about preaching. "Preachers?" he gasped, his voice cracking, his face turning pale in panic.

Dr. Minder noticed Billy's reaction and directed his comments to him. "Yes, Billy. I'm speaking at the men's mission. Would you like to come along?"

"Speaking?"

Still standing within inches of Billy's face, Emily asked, "Do you have a problem 'speaking'?"

"Um, no," Billy stammered, "but . . ."

"I'm Emily," the dark-haired beauty offered.

"I'm Speaking—I mean, I'm *Billy*."

Standing nearby, the always sophisticated Charles Massey found the perfect opportunity to airily interject: "And I am Charles Massey." He looked directly into Emily's eyes, ignoring Billy altogether.

"Hello, Charles Massey," Emily responded in a friendly tone.

"Hello, Emily. And Dr. Minder"—Charles turned toward the professor—"if *Mr. Speaking* doesn't wish to preach, I would love to give it a go."

Dr. Minder eyed Charles carefully. "We'll see, Charles," he said. "And, Billy, don't worry; if you don't want to speak at the mission, you can help serve dinners."

"Thank you, sir," Billy replied. "Dinners or speaking, you can count on me, Emily. I mean, Dr. Minder."

Emily smiled; she looked at Billy, next at Charles, then sauntered slowly from the room.

"Smooth," T. W. whispered to Billy. "That really went well."

Billy raised his brow in response.

A few days later, while working at the institute's cafeteria kitchen, Billy was carrying a large stack of dirty dishes toward the sink when he suddenly saw Emily. He smiled nervously and tried to tip the baseball hat covering his wavy hair, but the motion upset the delicate balance of plates stacked on his tray. Billy slipped and fell, with dishes, cups, saucers, and silverware clattering to the linoleum, creating a loud *CRASH!* and sending shattered glass in several directions at once.

Emily tried desperately to contain her laughter, to no avail. Several other students sitting nearby were snickering too, while some of Billy's buddies hooted out loud. T. W. saw the accident and hurried to help Billy clean up the mess. "Nice move, slick. That really got her attention."

Billy scowled at T. W., attempting to hide his embarrassment.

"I think he's fallen for you, Emily," Charles chortled when he saw what had happened.

T. W. scooped up some of the food from the floor and stood menacingly in front of Charles, holding the food in front of his face. "Have you eaten yet?" T. W. growled in defense of Billy.

"Don't even think about it!" Charles said hotly.

Billy got up off his knees, remnants of food and dregs of drinks clinging to his stained pants. He quickly stepped between T. W. and Charles to restrain his friend. "It's okay, T. W. It's okay," he said.

Charles glowered at Billy and T. W. "If either of you boys want a how-to lesson in Preaching 101, come to my room anytime—day or night."

"Well, it just so happens that Dr. Minder asked me to preach next Sunday at Bostwick Baptist Church," Billy taunted.

T. W. looked at Billy as though he had lost his mind. "He did? I thought you said—"

Billy cut him off. "Yes! I said . . ."

"Right," T. W. said mischievously. "You're preaching at Bostwick Baptist."

While the two boys enjoyed their chicanery, they failed to notice Emily sneaking admiring glances at Charles Massey. Her eyes sparkled, and she was smiling. It was clear that she wasn't thinking about anyone preaching.

❧

Saying that he would preach was one thing; actually preparing to preach was more study, tension, and work than Billy ever anticipated. He paced around his dormitory room, racking his brain, thinking of various sermon ideas; he spent hours reading, studying, and making notes. T. W. tried to help, mostly by encouraging his friend. "Don't worry, Billy. You'll do fine."

"But I don't know the first thing about preaching!" Billy fretted.

"Do you remember how enthusiastic you were while spreading the good news about Fuller brushes?" T. W. asked. "Well, preaching is spreading the good news about God's love. A much easier sale, if you ask me."

Billy took out a pad and scribbled down a few more notes. "Okay, okay. Sin. In the Greek, it is the word *metanoia*. It means missing the mark. It's as though you were shooting an arrow at a target, but you fell short. You missed the mark."

T. W. rubbed his chin, unimpressed. "Yeah. Missing the mark . . ."

The next morning, Billy was up early . . . pacing the hallway, preaching out loud, practicing his sermon ideas, while male students in various stages of undress moved to and from the communal bathroom and shower, yawning, rubbing their bleary eyes. Some who passed Billy tried to ignore him. Others laughed at him outright.

Thinking out loud, Billy said, "For all have sinned," as a fellow student, towel wrapped around his waist, passed by him. "No, 'For *all* have sinned,'" Billy repeated, shifting the emphasis. He hurriedly grabbed his towel and washcloth and stepped into the shower, still practicing his sermon as the water streamed down over his head. "Enter through the narrow gate," he said as the water cascaded over his body, his arms gesturing wildly. He was still preaching to himself when he stepped out of the shower and over to the steam-covered mirror. "'For wide is the gate. Broad is the road' . . . It's *terrible*! I can't do this!" he yelled.

T. W. had just ambled into the shower room and was standing at a sink, preparing to shave, when he heard Billy's outburst. "Yeah. Prob'ly right," he said to himself as much as to Billy.

❧

The night before he was to go along with Dean John Minder, Billy could barely sleep. Nevertheless, he was up early, showered, and ready to go several hours prior to the service. He dressed in his very best suit and tie and stepped in front of a wall mirror. "Just breathe," he told himself as he struggled to tame his pounding heart as much as his unruly hair.

Smoothing down the waves in his hair, he practiced his memorized Scripture verses. "'The way is broad . . . that leads to destruction,'" he said, looking in the mirror. He glanced at his watch and saw that it was time to go. He picked up the large stack of notes that he had settled on after much deliberation all week long. "This'll take at least two hours, T. W.," Billy said hopefully.

Bored stiff from listening to Billy's practice, T. W. didn't answer. He had slid down and fallen asleep in his chair.

Billy looked over and saw T. W. dozing. "Great. I put him to sleep," he said with a shrug.

❧

Bostwick Baptist Church was a quaint but charming white-framed country church, complete with a picturesque steeple. The old bell hanging in the steeple could still be rung when calling the congregation to assemble or celebrating weddings or national holidays, such as Independence Day, Memorial Day, or Armistice Day, the national holiday commemorating the end of World War I.

Billy and T. W. approached the door of the church as though they were bank robbers sneaking up on a safe. Few bank robbers entered the bank, however, carrying a stack of handwritten sermon notes. Billy's expression changed from excitement to one of raw nervous energy as he put his hand on the doorknob . . . and then stopped. His countenance dropped, and he turned to T. W. "I can't do it."

"You can!" T. W. reassured him.

Billy stared at the door, nervous and afraid of what might lie beyond it. "No, I can't." He backed away.

"Yes, you can, Billy." T. W. nudged his friend toward the door.

"'And many enter through it,'" Billy said aloud. He started to pull open the door, but then, seeing his reflection in the door's window, he suddenly remembered the baseball cap he had put on before leaving the dormitory. He quickly pulled off the hat and took a last moment to primp in the window, flattening his hair one last time. Just as Billy was about to pull open the door, someone opened it from the inside, and Billy lurched forward, nearly falling into the church.

He caught his balance and looked up, greeted by the congregation's loud singing of the gospel favorite, "I'd Rather Have Jesus." A middle-aged man who looked more like a cowboy than a minister was standing on the platform, waving his arms, directing the congregational singing.

Billy looked at T. W. as if to say, *Are you sure about this?* and T. W. gave him a playful shove forward. Billy inched his way toward the front of the church, passing by a large potbellied stove sitting right in the middle of the room. Dean Minder, already seated near the front, turned and saw Billy, and gave him an affirming nod. Billy was relieved to see the professor, and he hastened to sit down beside him just as the song finished.

Still standing in the aisle, T. W. looked to his right and spotted an empty seat. "I'll just sit . . . over here," he said.

Serving as the master of ceremonies, the cowboy singer stood casually on the platform. "And let's see who we have on the roster today," he said. "Ah . . ." He paused to put on pair of bifocals before reading from a large sheet of paper. "Let's see here. Coming all the way from Florida Bible Institute to offer us words of inspiration is a Mr. William Frank Graham." The cowboy looked up over the bifocals, searching for the speaker of the day.

"Billy, sir!" Billy spoke up from where he was seated with Dean Minder. "Just Billy."

The cowboy song leader had a good sense of humor. Or maybe he had just seen a number of nervous preacher boys. "Okay, folks," he said with a grin. "Welcome 'Just Billy.'"

Laughter rippled through the audience.

Billy looked sideways at Dr. Minder, wondering if this was really his introduction. Dr. Minder gave him an encouraging nod as the song leader took his seat, spitting in a large brass spittoon conveniently located beside his chair just off the platform.

Meanwhile, Billy anxiously gathered his stack of notes. Leaving his baseball cap on his chair, he hastily mounted the platform. Nervously, he approached the pulpit, perspiration already glistening on his forehead. He placed his notes on the pulpit and wiped his sweaty hands on his pant leg. Stepping closer to the podium, he spread out his large pile of notes, hoping they were in the correct order before he began.

The stack of notes startled the audience. Eyebrows rose all over the room as the congregation feared the worst. Several people glanced at one another, hoping to make a quick exit if the preacher grew too long-winded.

Billy looked up as though noticing the congregation for the first time. To his absolute amazement and joy, he saw Emily sitting in one of the pews near the front!

Billy took several deep breaths, trying to calm his nerves; his heart was thumping so loudly he was sure that the people sitting on the front pews could hear it.

From his position down front, the cowboy piped up, "You 'bout ready, son?"

Surprised, Billy responded, "For what?"

The congregation rippled with laughter once again.

"Oh. Oh, ready." He shifted his position behind the pulpit. "Yes. I'm ready." Billy anxiously looked at the clock on the wall, noting the time: noon exactly. Clearing his throat and then moistening his lips, he began.

He heard himself speaking, but it sounded almost as if another person was talking—very loudly, very rapidly, and *very* awkwardly, all punctuated with multiple gestures.

"Sin is missing the mark!" Billy barked, his voice escalating in tone as well as volume. He was on a roll, firing volley after volley from his voluminous notes at the shell-shocked congregation.

The audience sat up, stunned, feeling almost assaulted by the young preacher's words. T. W. watched and listened in awe, barely believing that the person speaking with such authority had been quivering in his shoes just a few minutes ago. Now, Billy was filled with the Spirit and speaking with persuasive passion, although his rapid-fire presentation made it difficult for anyone to actually absorb what he was saying!

In between bursts of vocal blasting, Billy peeked a quick glance at Emily. She caught his eye and tried to smile, despite her mind reeling from his verbal onslaught.

"The Greek word for sin is *metanoia*," Billy continued, flying through his notes. "Like an arrow aimed at a target, yet missing the bull's-eye!"

Several ranchers sat in a sort of awe, their mouths wide-open as they struggled to keep up. A number of women around the room tried equally as desperately to follow Billy's roller-coaster ride, their eyes and mouths agape in wonder as Billy moved at light-speed, turning his pages and delivering the goods.

From his perspective, Dr. Minder observed Billy carefully,

smiling to himself from time to time at Billy's youthful zeal and exuberance. Yes, Billy Graham had much to learn about the art of preaching. Yet the veteran preaching instructor recognized that Billy possessed "something else" as well. Despite Dean Minder's attempts to remain impassive and objective, he repeatedly found himself being struck by Billy, drawn in, not simply to his message, but to his heart's desire to communicate the timeless truths of the Bible. The dean had seen hundreds of young preachers . . . yet there was something different about this one . . .

"We have all missed the mark with God!" Billy's voice snapped Dean Minder out of his reverie.

At the pulpit, pages were flying again, and Billy was plowing on, covering the Bible from Genesis to Revelation, more determined than ever and getting even louder as he spoke. "And that's about all I know about the 144,000 in the book of Revelation," said Billy almost apologetically, before pausing long enough for a breath.

Dr. Minder grinned slightly, trying to smother his own laughter.

The clock on the wall now read 12:04, and the cowboy sat back deeply in his chair as though hanging on for dear life. Surely the preacher boy had to slow down soon, didn't he?

He didn't.

Quite the contrary, Billy caught a fresh wind, and pages began to fly even faster. "And then there was Jonah, who was given the job to warn Nineveh," Billy continued. The congregation listened politely, trying to follow Billy's madcap race through the Scripture. Billy continued dogmatically, regarding Jonah's less-than-willing performance at Nineveh. "And he didn't even want to do it!"

Dr. Minder rubbed his chin thoughtfully as he listened to his student preaching. The dean was touched by Billy's zeal and found himself rooting for the young man all the more.

Billy continued turning the pages of his notes. "And what about David, and Moses?" Billy asked, suddenly gesturing strongly, thrusting his long arms into the air, stunning the crowd into a collective near gasp. There was no need to answer Billy's rhetorical question; he was already miles down the "Roman Road," preparing to challenge his listeners on the most crucial issue of all—salvation. "Is there anyone here who thinks they have not sinned?" he asked, pausing for effect. "YOU NEED CHRIST!" he shouted.

Done! The pile of notes was completely turned over. Billy had sailed through them all, from the Old Testament to the New, and back and forth again. He sheepishly turned his head and looked up at the clock on the wall, fearing he may have preached much too long. The clock now read 12:08.

Billy blinked hard and looked at the hands on the clock again. Sure enough, he had preached for a grand total of eight minutes! He looked down at his stack of notes and realized that he had exhausted not only all of his notes but pretty much everything he knew about the Bible as well. He glanced at the clock again and back at his notes as a look of deep consternation crept over his countenance.

Seated in the congregation, T. W. recognized what was happening. He leapt to his feet and shouted, "Hallelujah! Amen!"

Everyone in the small church—including the preacher— turned to look at T. W.

Embarrassed, T. W. touched his hand to his heart. "I'm sitting down now," he said quietly, nodding to the congregation. As T. W. slowly sank back into his seat, Billy looked out quickly to see if Emily was still there. She was. And better yet, she was all smiles!

Billy hurriedly darted to his seat and sat down, out of breath, his back flat against the back of the pew.

The congregation seemed to express a communal sigh of relief too, now that the novice preacher had concluded his message. The good-natured cowboy song leader jumped to his feet and stood behind the vacated pulpit. "Well! Mr. Graham! You sure gave yourself a workout!" he said with a grin. "And us too! Thank you so much for coming and preachin' the word. And, uh . . . for bein' so quick 'bout it."

Billy nodded toward the cowboy. Seated next to him in the pew, Dr. Minder leaned over, placed his hand on Billy's shoulder, and whispered, "Billy, I can't wait to see what God is going to do with you."

Billy looked his professor in the eyes. "Do you mean that . . . in a good way?"

Dr. Minder nearly laughed aloud. "Yes, Billy. In a *very* good way."

Billy's hands were still shaking as he reached out to grasp Dr. Minder's extended hand. He was exhilarated and exhausted, and he had been undeniably stung by the preaching bug. Billy turned to find T. W.'s face in the congregation—and his friend gave him an enthusiastic thumbs-up.

Billy was thrilled that Dean Minder had complimented him so kindly, and he was happy to know that his friend was proud of him too, but there was yet another person's approval he was seeking.

Chapter Six

The cafeteria at the Florida Bible Institute was a relatively small room, part of what was once a restaurant at the country club, so it was nearly impossible to be inconspicuous, even if a person wanted to be alone. The day after Billy preached for the first time at Bostwick Baptist Church, he was carrying his tray when he spied Emily reading a book while eating her lunch, and she was sitting all alone.

Billy approached her table and stood behind the empty seat across from her. "May I?" he asked courteously.

Emily looked up from her book, appearing surprised. She smiled at Billy and nodded sweetly. "Sure. Do you eat as fast as you preach?" she asked, a twinkle in her eye.

Billy feigned ignorance. "You were there?" He placed his hand on his chest as if he were having a heart attack, then placed his tray on the table.

Emily cocked her head to one side and looked up at Billy demurely. "I was sure you noticed."

"I did notice," Billy said sheepishly. "I just . . . well, it could've been—no, it was you. Yup. You were there. It was most definitely you." Embarrassed, Billy turned his red face away from Emily and saw T. W., who was again giving Billy his trademark thumbs-up.

"I thought . . ."

"Yeah?" Billy asked hopefully.

Emily looked him in the eyes as she spoke. "I thought you did a . . . good job."

"Really?"

Emily smiled slightly. "Really."

Billy turned his back on Emily momentarily so he could secretly give T. W. a return gesture. He then pulled his chair in front of Emily, sat down, and enjoyed the best meal he had eaten since he arrived at the institute, though he would have been hard-pressed to remember a thing he ate. Billy was smitten.

After preaching his first sermon, Billy was even more focused on his studies. He knew his time of preparation might be limited, so he wanted to learn as much about the Bible, and how to present its message, as he possibly could in the short time he would be at Florida Bible Institute. Each day, he listened attentively with renewed interest to his professors. He was energized, committed, drawn in, and he eagerly took notes in every class. He especially enjoyed Dr. Minder's class on evangelism.

Following Billy's preaching debut, one day during class, Dr. Minder walked to the chalkboard and again slowly wrote the word *Evangelist* on the black slate. "An evangelist," he said, as he turned around to see his students' response, "is a person who brings good news, the good news of the gospel."

Billy's mind was racing. He raised his hand to ask a question. "Yes, Billy?"

"Who becomes an evangelist?" Billy asked passionately. "Is desire enough? Is devotion enough? Is commitment to selfless service enough?"

"Good questions, Billy," Dr. Minder replied. "For one, you must develop oratorical skills. And it cannot and must not be about money or fame. It's about the Call. It's about serving the One who died for you. It's about His message."

Billy listened intently, the professor's words igniting a fire in his soul that seemed to set his entire life ablaze. Other class members nodded in agreement. Some looked intently at their Bibles; still others simply stared nonplussed into the professor's face. But for Billy, Dean Minder's words were a revelation. He took them to heart and focused even more on how he could become not merely a better preacher but an evangelist.

From that moment on, he practiced preaching anywhere and everywhere. Walking acoss campus, he preached to the shrubbery, the light posts, imaginary people and real ones too, enthusiastically sharing his message, always loudly, gesturing awkwardly at first, then slowly but surely finding ways to punctuate his points. Sometimes he placed his arms behind his back as he spoke; at other times he drew his arms in and folded them across his chest. Occasionally, he placed his thumb under his chin, with his index finger curled around it, in a thoughtful pose that would one day become a style imitated by thousands of young preachers.

Walking from class to class, Billy rehearsed. "Will you come to Christ?" he'd ask aloud, posing the question to nobody in particular as students passed by him in wonderment, gazing at him as though he had lost his senses. A group of attractive young women approached, but Billy kept right on preaching, not even noticing that one of the women trying *not* to notice him was Emily. Billy simply preached on as Emily passed by, frowning, shaking her head, and looking toward the ground.

"Will you give your life to Him?" Billy asked as several male students followed just behind the young women. Charles Massey chortled as Billy passed. "Somebody put him out of his misery," he mocked.

Several students walking with Charles laughed and shook their heads, but Emily turned around and spoke emphatically. "Everybody has to start somewhere."

"Well, he's at the starting line," Charles quipped. "That's for sure. But I can't see him finishing one full lap." The students on the sidewalk laughed again as Billy, still in his own world, continued on his way, still practicing his preaching, swinging his long arms at the wind in his wide, sweeping gestures.

℃

Charles kept up his subtle and sometimes not-so-subtle efforts to undermine Billy's budding relationship with Emily. At a campus game day, his ploy proved much more overt. Billy and Emily were playing croquet against Charles and his partner. A number of other students and faculty members, including Dr. Minder, stood by watching, awaiting their turn to play.

"Is that your ball, Billy?" Charles asked, pointing at Billy's green-striped ball sitting within scoring position.

"You know it is," Billy replied.

Charles smiled fiendishly. He looked up at Billy, then over at Emily, and then in a firm pendulum stroke, swinging the mallet deeply between his legs, Charles blasted his ball expertly through a wicket, smashing into Billy's ball, driving it off course and out of scoring position. Emily couldn't help herself; she stood with one hand on her hip, gazing admiringly at Charles, impressed with his savvy. Charles looked up at her and flashed a handsome smile. Although they didn't say anything to each other, Billy noticed the interchange.

"*Croquet*, huh?" he muttered. "How 'bout a little baseball?"

೧

While Charles was busy trying to demean Billy in Emily's eyes, Billy continued to practice his preaching everywhere he went. One spring day, Billy was at the zoo, standing in front of the cages and looking at the animals. Suddenly he wheeled around and unloaded on the elephant. "Make a decision to follow Him!" he challenged the huge beast. "What is stopping you? Will you be saved?"

The elephant and all of the other animals just stared at Billy, while a few looked away, apparently unmoved. "Well, if you burn in hell, don't blame me. You were warned."

The elephant let out a loud blast with his trunk, startling Billy so much he nearly jumped out of his shoes. "Okay, okay. I stepped over the line. I admit it. I'll let God decide who goes to heaven and who goes to hell."

One day, as Billy was going past the campus chapel, he decided to stop and practice his preaching for a while. He opened the doors and stepped inside the cool, dimly lit, empty chapel. Once on the platform, Billy preached with great zeal, loudly and awkwardly pleading to empty pews. "Christ came to give us new life . . . and hope," he said, raising his voice as he swept his arm in a huge gesticulation, "as we give our lives to Him!"

An elderly custodian sweeping at the back of the chapel stopped, leaned on his broom handle, and listened to Billy for a few minutes.

"Will you give your life to Him?" Billy implored the invisible congregation in the empty seats.

The custodian continued sweeping, working his way to the front of the chapel as Billy concluded his "sermon." The custodian paused, leaned on the broom again, and looked up at Billy, still behind the pulpit.

"Son, I've seen the greatest preachers of the day," the custodian said. "They've all come through here, and they all have one thing in common . . . talent. So I can spot it when I see it."

Billy looked at the custodian expectantly, ready to receive the compliment, even if offered by the janitor.

"And trust me when I say this," the custodian continued. "Son, *you ain't got it.*"

℘

A few days later, Billy was at the florist's, looking at corsages through the glass of a refrigerated case. "Corsages are all twenty-five cents," the florist offered. "Fifty cents for something extra special."

"I'll take a fifty-cent corsage," Billy said boldly.

The florist raised his eyebrows approvingly. "A special lady?" he asked.

Billy could feel his face warming. "Special? As in . . ."

"Special," the florist said with slight nod and the look of a romanticist.

"Oh," Billy responded. "'Special.' Yes. Very."

The florist smiled and carefully removed one of the expensive corsages from the case, delicately placing it in a small box with a plastic window, through which Billy could admire his purchase.

The party in the Florida Bible Institute gathering room was in full swing by the time Billy arrived. The room was decorated with colored lights, balloons, and a long, paper-covered table lined with punch bowls, fruit, and pastries. A sharply dressed "big band" played favorites such as "Stardust" and hits of the crooners from the 1920s and '30s.

Billy had dressed in his best suit and tie and appeared quite dapper as he entered the room, carrying his "special" corsage. With the lights down low, it took a minute or so before Billy's eyes adjusted enough for him to search the faces, looking for Emily.

When he finally spotted her, Billy's face flushed crimson red. Emily was sitting beside Charles, engaged in close conversation, and she was already wearing the same fifty-cent corsage that Billy carried in his hands. Innocently confused, he quickly hid his corsage behind his back and strode across the room to approach Emily for an explanation. Out of the corner of her eye, Emily saw Billy heading in her direction, and as he neared her, she rose to meet him. "Good evening, Billy," she greeted him cheerfully, though somewhat awkwardly.

Billy couldn't help staring at the corsage Emily was wearing. He tried to speak, but nothing made sense. "Hi . . . I, uh . . . I thought . . ."

Emily broke in, "Billy, I need to talk to you." She glanced at Charles, who was looking down at the floor. "Come with me," she said, looking up again into Billy's face. Then she sweetly guided him to a private corner of the room.

When they were away from most of the others at the party, Emily turned toward Billy, reaching out and holding one of his arms, but keeping their bodies well apart.

"Billy," she began softly, "I'm in love with Charles."

The words hit Billy like a lightning bolt, searing through his heart and mind. Surely she was joking. Surely this was a colossal mistake. He felt the sensation of Emily's hand on his arm, and suddenly the corsage he carried in his other hand felt like a fifty-pound weight. This couldn't be happening. Billy looked into Emily's lovely face, his own face streaked with pain.

Emily's voice turned more businesslike. "He's going to Harvard."

"So?" Billy protested.

"So, I want to marry someone who's going to do something special with his life."

"'Special'?"

Emily hesitated, then took a deep breath and exhaled slowly, almost sighing. "Billy, you're a nice fellow. I like you. But . . ."

"But what?"

"I just don't think you're going to amount to much," Emily blurted. "I'm sorry." Emily turned abruptly and walked away, leaving Billy standing there, holding his corsage.

At just the wrong time, T. W. bounded up to him. "Hey, big guy. How're ya doin', lucky ducky?"

Billy spun on his heel and walked away without a word, leaving T. W. standing alone.

"Was it something I said?"

Chapter Seven

In the starkly decorated hospital room, the aged Charles Templeton shook his head sadly. Templeton looked up at Deborah Matthews as though trying to help her understand. "Ha! While I was converting thousands, Billy was swatting mosquitoes," he said.

"Really? What do you mean?" Deborah asked. "Please keep going."

Templeton looked at her as though she were an ignoramus. "I had greatness written on my forehead!" he said adamantly. "Billy had average written on his." He paused and looked away for a moment, then brought his gaze back to the camera. "I'm sorry," he said quietly. "I didn't mean . . . You can edit that part out, correct?"

"Absolutely. We'll edit that out," Deborah lied. She turned and whispered to the camera operator, "Go in tighter."

"Any tighter and we'd only have nose hairs," the camera operator whispered back to her.

Templeton sat up straighter in his bed and fluffed the blankets covering his legs. "Billy was a good man. A very good young man. That's what I was getting at," he said sincerely.

ↄ৲

FLORIDA BIBLE INSTITUTE, 1938

Out on the golf course in the spring of 1938, Billy wasn't so sure about being good. What did it get a person, anyhow? Nothing but rejection. He walked slowly in the moonlight, his tie loosened, kicking the dirt as he went; he was deeply distressed. He stopped beside the pond and stared out at the water. Seeing his own reflection in the moonlit water, he realized that he was still clutching the corsage tenaciously, unwilling to let go of it, as though if he held on to it tighter, Emily might come back to him. Finally, he took a last look at the corsage, turned, and tossed it into the water. The sweet-smelling spray made a plopping sound as it punctured the glassy surface of the pond, then popped back up to the surface and began drifting . . . drifting . . . slowly drifting away. Billy watched with a pained expression as he let Emily float out of his life.

Vera Resue, not Billy, was the valedictorian of Billy's 1940 graduating class at Florida Bible Institute. Although Billy had applied himself fastidiously to his studies, he was not an academic. Even his interest in learning how to preach had only one purpose—to bring people into a relationship with God.

Vera's speech on Class Night, just before commencement that

spring, possessed little of the usual optimistic, bright-eyed look at the future often heard at graduation ceremonies. Indeed, it was difficult to be lightheartedly positive in 1939, with war clouds looming over much of Europe and the Far East. Perhaps that is why Vera's speech took more of a somber, almost prophetic tone. Speaking of the encroaching darkness in the world, Vera reminded her listeners that current events had not taken God by surprise. Indeed, He always had a plan. "Each time, God has a chosen human instrument to shine forth His light in the darkness," she encouraged the tightly packed crowd of students dressed in commencement caps and gowns, as well as a few family members clad in their Sunday best. The audience listened intently, their faces showing the burden of the times, but their hearts buoyed by Vera's hopeful reminder.

Vera looked at the addressees and spoke more prophetically than she realized. "It has been said that Luther revolutionized the world. Yet it was not he, but Christ working through him. The time is ripe for another Luther, another Wesley, another Moody." Her eyes panned the room, connecting with several of the graduates who were sitting on the edges of their chairs, inspired, as if their names should be the next ones added to Vera's list. Billy, however, sat with his head bowed, unpretentious, hardly daring to assume that God could do anything great through him. After all, he had been told many times that he was a failure, that he'd never be a great preacher—or amount to much of anything at all. He held few lofty ambitions and no illusions of grandeur as he listened to Vera conclude her remarks.

"There is room for another name on this list of visionaries. Who will it be?" she asked.

☙

TEMPLETON'S HOSPITAL ROOM, 2001

"Who, indeed?" Charles Templeton boomed with such intensity, his nurse peeked inside the doorway, just to make sure he was okay.

"Who will it be?" he repeated to Deborah Matthews, but it was obvious he was watching his own mental movie again. The reporter didn't interrupt him; instead, Deborah simply rolled her finger toward the cameramen. "Keep rolling," she mouthed to him.

☙

VARIOUS STADIUMS IN THE UNITED STATES AND CANADA, FALL 1940

In the mid-1940s, as World War II was drawing to a bloody, bitterly fought end, a crowd of more than ten thousand people poured into an arena in America's Midwest. The master of ceremonies approached the podium microphone, leaned into it, and above the din of the crowd, belted out, "Ladies and gentlemen . . ."

The large crowd quickly drew quiet, respectfully awaiting the emcee's introduction. "Ladies and gentlemen, I present to you . . . Charles Templeton!" The crowd erupted in a roar usually reserved for sports superstars or presidential candidates.

Another night, another sports arena, this time with more than twenty thousand people jammed inside, another emcee repeated this performance. A month later, in another city, another stadium, the adoring crowds had swelled to more than thirty thousand people. "Ladies and gentlemen, I present to you . . . Charles Templeton!"

The audience burst into applause as young, handsome, debonair Charles Templeton—Chuck, as he preferred to be called—bolted onto the stage, waving to the crowd. Although his dark eyes were nearly blinded by the thousands of flashbulbs going off in his face, Templeton didn't seem to mind. He smiled and waved, his dark brown hair perfectly in place as he walked first to one side of the stage, then to the other, his large, athletic body moving with the control and grace of a ballet dancer. Nattily dressed in a well-tailored, dark suit with a loud, bold print tie, Templeton looked part businessman, part politician, and part showman.

He was accustomed to speaking before large crowds now, having drawn more than eighteen thousand people to Toronto's Maple Leaf Gardens and equally large crowds in various cities across the United States. But it hadn't always been that way. Shortly after leaving his thriving career as a sports cartoonist, Chuck had joined the Church of the Nazarene, where his reputation as a well-known artist was redirected. He was often asked to present a biblical message through his sketches and soon became known as something of a novelty, a "sketch evangelist," within the small denomination. He frequently presented "chalk talks" to young people, retelling a Bible story while he swiftly and expertly re-created the biblical scene on an artist's drawing board in front of his audience. Most of this work he did for free, or at best a pittance, since money was not really an allurement to him.

In 1936, an itinerant evangelist invited Chuck to accompany him to Lowville, New York, for two weeks of evangelistic meetings in which Chuck would provide biblically based sketches and lead the singing. Chuck crossed the U.S. and Canadian border with a bus ticket and only $1.67 in his pocket. The U.S. Immigrations officer was reluctant to allow Chuck into the country. "We got plenty of unemployed people here already," he commented caustically as he stamped Templeton's immigration form.

But Templeton's ignominy and obscurity were soon dispelled as he began preaching anywhere anyone would have him—and many congregations wanted him, as his fame spread on both sides of the border. Although he had only a ninth-grade education, his denomination—more concerned about "anointing" and orthodoxy than academic degrees—ordained him as a minister of the gospel, and Templeton was on his way.

He preached on street corners, in tar-papered shacks, at outdoor camp meetings, in storefront churches, anywhere two or three people gathered together to hear the gospel. He preached in 110-degree heat in Paris, Kentucky, near Lexington, and he preached in the freezing cold of northern Ontario. Charles Templeton was committed to preaching the gospel anywhere anyone wanted to hear it—and thousands of people did. Soon he was drawing large crowds in both Canada and the United States. Crowds sometimes as large as forty thousand people, standing on their feet and applauding, greeted him when he bounded onto the platforms. Newspaper headlines touted him as "The Man Who Speaks for God."

But did he?

Chapter Eight

A small group of men, all spiritual leaders—some pastors, a few simple farmers—gathered around Billy Graham on the cramped platform of Peniel Baptist Church, not far from Florida Bible Institute, in February 1939. The men had taken care to dress in a manner fitting for such a solemn occasion, several of them wearing their suit coats atop their overalls. Billy had been preaching in various parts of western Florida while at Florida Bible Institute, so most of the men had heard him and had seen how people responded to his messages of salvation. A Presbyterian all his life, Billy had decided to be ordained—dedicated to God and licensed for ministry by a governing church body—by an association of Southern Baptists, the denomination in which he was preaching most frequently.

Following the perfunctory greetings and sharing of background information, the group of Southern Baptist leaders got down to business, questioning Billy about his beliefs as well as his desire to preach. At the close of the session, the men approved Billy for ordination.

That same night, during a regularly scheduled church service, Billy humbly knelt on the platform, and the group of elders laid their strong, calloused hands on his shoulders. Dr. Minder stepped up behind Billy, placed his hands on Billy's head, and prayed an ordination prayer over him. Dr. Minder then declared, "William Franklin Graham, you are now ordained as a servant of Christ." When Billy stood to his feet, he was an ordained minister, legally permitted to perform weddings, conduct funerals, serve Communion, and perform other ministerial roles besides preaching. The ordination did not give him some special privilege or position; it simply ratified the position Billy had already taken —that of a servant.

Later that evening, Billy and T. W. sat on the steps outside the chapel. They weren't really talking; they were simply looking at and listening to God's magnificent creation, enjoying the extraordinary sights and sounds He had built into it. After a while, Billy spoke up quietly, "I sure wish my momma coulda been here today."

T. W. nodded. "I know she's real proud of you, Billy. Real proud."

⅋

TEMPLETON'S HOSPITAL ROOM, 2001

In Charles Templeton's hospital room, the subject of the documentary suddenly turned sullen. "Billy Graham was going nowhere," he said.

"Going nowhere?" Deborah Matthews repeated a bit incredulously.

Templeton nodded his head slowly. "I can't explain it," he practically whispered. "'Puff Graham.'" He paused and looked up at the reporter. "That's what I heard."

The female interviewer seemed confused. "Puff Graham?" she asked.

"What?" Templeton acted as though she had awakened him from a deep sleep.

"What does 'Puff Graham' mean?" Deborah asked.

ↄ

WHEATON, ILLINOIS, FALL 1940

A leaf floating on the wind drifted across the sidewalk; a portion of a Chicago newspaper with Charles Templeton's photograph on the front page blew past the walk as well, caught in the brisk fall breeze. The newsprint flipped and fluttered and flew up against an off-white brick wall on which the words *Wheaton College* could be read.

Wheaton College, a small liberal arts institution located about twenty-five miles west of Chicago, was founded just prior to the Civil War as a place of academic excellence that would hold true to the Holy Scriptures. Over the years it remained a staunch bulwark of evangelical faith and a formidable intellectual opponent of the creeping theological liberalism that tended to denigrate belief in the Bible as God's Word, often to the point of considering the Gospels nothing more than a series of stories fabricated by fertile human imaginations.

Billy had been aware of Wheaton prior to attending Florida Bible Institute, but the tuition costs and the distance from his family in North Carolina—not to mention Billy's less-than-stellar academic performance in high school—placed the school out of his reach. But in the summer of 1939, when John Minder decided to take some time away from his church, Tampa Gospel Tabernacle, he invited Billy to serve as his summer replacement, preaching at all the services and carrying out the normal duties of a pastor. Billy jumped at the chance.

Two businessmen visited Florida Bible Institute during a vacation, and while there, they heard Billy preach. One of the men was attorney Paul Fischer, and the other, Elner Edman, was the brother of Wheaton's president, V. Raymond Edman. When Paul and Elner suggested that Billy would benefit from further training at Wheaton, Billy couldn't have agreed more. Yet he knew he could not afford the four-year, fully accredited college.

Paul astonished Billy by offering to pay Billy's first-year tuition fees at Wheaton, and Elner offered to help with other expenses. Billy applied to the prestigious school and was accepted. He could hardly believe it!

At nearly twenty-two years of age, Billy drove to Wheaton in September 1940 to begin college. Many of his credits from Florida Bible Institute did not transfer fully to Wheaton, so although he was a little older than most of his classmates, he began school as a second-semester freshman, almost starting over from scratch. He chose to major in anthropology, the study of man. But it wasn't his study of man at Wheaton that changed Billy's life dramatically; it was the study of woman, one woman in particular.

⟡

The chapel bell sounded, and suddenly an empty stairwell became chaotic and clogged with students hurrying up and down the staircase. Billy, the fastest of all, came flying down the stairwell. As he ran, the sight of a beautiful young woman caught him off guard; he was so instantly enamored of her radiant beauty that he nearly tripped and fell. The young woman stopped, and for a moment, her eyes followed Billy down the stairs. She turned to proceed on her way up the stairwell, when she felt a tap on her shoulder.

"Excuse me, but I think you dropped this," Billy said, holding up a thin note tablet that had slipped out from under her arm.

"Oh. Thank you," the young woman responded gratefully, taking the tablet from his outstretched hand.

"You're welcome," Billy said, and in his usual rapid-fire delivery, added, "and you are the prettiest young woman I have ever laid eyes on."

"Oh. Thank you . . . again," the beauty replied.

"You're welcome again. Bye." Billy bounded back down the stairs, then stopped and looked back up at her. "I'm Billy. Billy Graham," he said.

"Nice to meet you, Billy Graham," the woman said sweetly. "I'm—"

"Ruth," Billy interrupted. "Bye again." Billy waved and was gone, around the corner of the staircase and on his way.

Ruth's roommate, Marjorie Bostrum, walked up to Ruth and nudged her. "He's been eyein' you for months," she said with a laugh.

Ruth smiled. "Yes, I know."

At the bottom of the stairs, Grady Wilson, whom Billy had talked into joining him at Wheaton, was waiting for him, nearly bursting with excitement. "Do you know who that is?" Grady asked.

"Yup."

"Every guy—"

"I know."

"Her parents are—"

"Missionaries in China. I know," Billy interjected.

"She's beautiful!"

"I know," Billy said with a mischievous smile.

❧

Attractive, intellectually bright, and quick to smile, Ruth Bell was indeed the woman every eligible young bachelor at Wheaton wanted to marry. She was also known for her spiritual depth, part of which, no doubt, resulted from her upbringing. She was the daughter of Presbyterian medical missionaries and had been born in China, where she lived her first seventeen years. Although her childhood had been happy and exhilarating, she had also experienced a great deal of heartache. She had witnessed natural disasters, such as devastating monsoons, as well as indescribable human-inflicted suffering; she was well aware of the 1937 Rape of Nanking carried out by the Imperial Japanese Army against China, resulting in some of the most atrocious examples of inhumanities ever known. If Ruth Bell had a seriousness and a maturity not shared by many of her classmates at Wheaton, she had good reason. She hoped one day to return to Tibet as a missionary, and she was willing to forgo marriage to do so, thinking that someday she, too, may be called upon to give her life as a martyr. Yet for all her seriousness, Ruth had a contagious personality and no shortage of friends, both male and female.

Billy had been infatuated with Ruth since the first day he saw her, but it seemed every time he got near her, his awkward side came to the fore. One day, when Billy and his friends, Howard, George, Grady, and Harvey, were helping another friend, Johnny Streater, move some furniture, Ruth passed by with her room-mate. Dressed in work clothes, Billy and Howard had just hoisted a large piece of heavy furniture as the women approached. Harvey spotted Ruth and let out a low whistle. Grady saw her too and whispered as loudly as possible, "Billy!"

Billy looked up from the piece of furniture, but he looked the wrong way. Howard tried to give Billy a heads-up. "Short stop. Left field," Howard hinted.

When Billy turned around and saw Ruth, he nearly dropped the piece of furniture he and Howard were carrying.

"That looks heavy," said Ruth as she drew near.

"No. I mean, yes," stammered Billy. "Not really. I have a note . . ."

"A note?" Ruth repeated inquisitively.

"A no—," Billy began but couldn't get the word to come out of his mouth. "Oh, nothin'. Wow. China, huh?"

"China?"

"And Japan." Billy was grasping for anything now. "And aren't those Australians an interesting bunch?"

The other guys pushed on with the load, and Billy staggered to keep up. Ruth walked on a little farther, then turned around and gave Billy a second look.

Meanwhile, Billy never took his eyes off her. He continued staring after her long after she had disappeared from sight. He was completely taken with her. When he and Howard finally put down the heavy piece of furniture, Billy reached inside his shirt pocket and took out a carefully folded note and held it close to his chest. "I am such an idiot," he said to himself.

Grady noticed Billy's actions. "What in the world is that?" he asked.

"I wrote her a note . . . a few weeks ago," Billy replied. "But I've been afraid to give it to her."

"You wrote her a note?"

"Yes, I wrote her a note," Billy said as they picked up the furniture again.

"Want me to give it to her?" Grady offered.

Eyes wide, Billy blurted, "Don't even think about it!"

The following day, as Billy was about to pay for his lunch in Wheaton's cafeteria, he turned to see Ruth seated at a table with Marjorie and a few other girls. Billy noticed an empty seat beside Ruth and decided to take a risk. Steeling his courage, he started over to Ruth's table when a handsome, athletic-looking young man plopped down in that very seat. Billy stopped in his tracks and veered away, taking a seat at another table across the room.

Disappointed, Billy took the note out of his pocket. Just then, he looked up and saw Marjorie standing nearby, looking in his direction and smiling! She waved, but Billy wasn't sure who she was waving at.

"Yes. I mean you!" Marjorie called out to Billy. She moved closer to his table. "We're in anthropology together. I sit behind you."

"Marjorie . . . Baker?" Billy asked.

"Bostrom. Close enough," she replied with a shrug.

Billy nervously played with the note in his hand. He looked

beyond Marjorie at Ruth; she seemed to be having a wonderful time chatting with the athletic guy. Billy was so entranced by Ruth that he didn't even notice Marjorie sitting down across from him. Billy leaned slightly to the right so he could see Ruth just past Marjorie's left ear.

"I liked what you had to say in class this week," Marjorie said. "Do you want to study together for the midterm? I could use the extra help." She smiled at Billy.

But Billy barely noticed. He continued to look past Marjorie, his gaze fixed on Ruth.

"Is there something wrong with my ear?" Marjorie asked.

"Your ear?"

Marjorie followed Billy's gaze, turning around in her chair, then turned back to Billy. "Is that a note?" she asked, pointing to the paper Billy was clutching so tightly.

"A note? Why would this be a note?" Billy responded nervously. "A note? Ha! No, no."

Marjorie looked at him and cocked her head to the side. "So what do you say? The library?"

"The library? A place with books," Billy stammered. "Where people study."

"Right-o," Marjorie answered with a smile.

Just then Billy's attention was distracted by another athletic guy who approached and stood next to Ruth's table, talking to her and the first fellow. Billy's eyes followed as Ruth stood up and headed out of the cafeteria. The two young men traipsed behind her, like puppies close on her heels, hanging on her every word.

"You seem to have a fascination with my roommate."

Billy blushed. "A fascination with . . . what? Ruth Bell is your *roommate*, Marjorie Bostrom?"

"Yes, she's quite popular with the boys," Marjorie said, "but they're barking up the wrong tree. Marriage isn't part of her life plan. She's going to be a missionary in Tibet. So how about tomorrow? After class."

"Tibet? What happened to China?" Billy asked innocently.

"China's still there," Marjorie replied with a hint of a smile.

"Right. Never moved," Billy said, embarrassed at his gaffe.

"Tomorrow?" Marjorie asked again.

"It's a date," beamed Billy.

"A study date," Marjorie corrected him.

"I'm really looking forward to it."

Marjorie smiled and picked up her books. "I really bet you are."

Chapter Nine

Marjorie Bostrom was not an unattractive young woman. Her only real disadvantage was being Ruth Bell's friend and roommate, which caused most young men to look past her. Perky, outgoing, and somewhat sassy, Marjorie didn't mind being Ruth's go-between. She knew her roommate well: no ordinary Wheaton male was going to sweep Ruth Bell off her feet or, more important, distract her from what she felt was her divine calling to lay down her life in service to God. So Marjorie enjoyed the repartee with the young men of Wheaton College, knowing full well that the attention they showered on her was meant for Ruth. She didn't mind. Not really. Besides, being second fiddle to Ruth afforded Marjorie the luxury of acting forward with the fellas on campus, without seeming like a flirtatious floozy.

Marjorie arrived first at the library in Blanchard Hall.

Choosing a large, rectangular table away from the main part of the room, where other students were busy studying, she spread out her study materials, sat down, and kept an eye out for Billy. She didn't have to wait long.

Within minutes after classes dismissed, Billy bounded into the library, books under his arm, and strode across the room with a smile on his face, his eyes searching for Marjorie. When he spotted her, he waved and headed straight for her table. He was disappointed that Ruth was not studying with her, but he made no reference to Marjorie's petite, vivacious roommate as he sat down and greeted his study companion.

"Hi, Billy," Marjorie whispered. "I'm glad you could come. That anthropology midterm is going to be a bear, and I can sure use some help."

"Hello, Marjorie," Billy boomed. "How are—"

"Shh!" at least half a dozen people around the room said simultaneously.

"Please keep your voices down," the librarian said with a dour look on her face. "People are trying to study."

Marjorie placed her index finger over her lips. Billy nodded and waved his hand in the air. He pulled his chair up to the table and opened his anthropology book in front of him. For the next half hour, he and Marjorie compared notes, whispered to each other about potential test questions, and silently read over important passages from their books. Marjorie was immersed in her reading, and Billy was almost starting to enjoy anthropology, when into the library walked Ruth Bell, wearing a winter beige dress, looking as stylish and sophisticated as ever. Billy stared at Ruth unabashedly as she took a seat facing him at a long study desk on the opposite side of the library.

Billy tried to refocus his attention on his study notes, but his eyes kept lifting off the pages in hopes of catching a glimpse of Ruth across the room. Unconsciously, Billy reached inside his shirt pocket and nervously began fumbling with the note that he had carried on his person for several weeks now.

Marjorie looked up and noticed that Billy's concentration had been broken. Instinctively, she turned around and, to no surprise, saw Ruth at the other end of the room. Marjorie turned back toward Billy, who was idly playing with the note. She grinned to herself and went back to work. A few minutes later, she saw Billy lower his book to the tabletop as he gave up reading anthropology and openly admired Ruth instead.

Marjorie sounded somewhat annoyed as she whispered, "Are you gonna study for the midterm or study Ruth?"

"Huh?"

Marjorie pointed to Billy's hand. "Is that a note?" she asked.

"A note? No. What note?"

Marjorie feigned disgust. "What are you, in fifth grade? You're wearin' all the letters off the page. Gimme that." She snatched the note out of Billy's hand.

"No. No!" Billy blurted, forgetting to whisper.

The librarian frowned, looked up from her desk, and glared at Billy and Marjorie. "Shh!" she hissed.

With whimsical defiance, Marjorie looked at the note, then at Billy. She pushed away from the table, marched over to Ruth, and slid the note toward her.

Ruth looked up from her studies, laid down her pencil, and took the note from her friend's hand. Without a word, Marjorie stretched out her arm and pointed straight back at Billy, who was now dying of embarrassment.

Ruth unfolded the note and began to read. Her eyes brightened, and a hint of a smile darted across her face. She looked up at Billy.

From across the room, Billy called out, "It's okay if you can't . . ."

Ruth smiled at him. "I'd love to," she called back to him.

The librarian was about to have a fit. "SHHHHHHH!" she hissed, even more loudly than before.

Marjorie marched back to Billy and sat down at their table. "Now can we study?" she asked.

The handwritten note that Billy had been carrying around for weeks was his boldest attempt at inviting Ruth to the Wheaton glee club's presentation of Handel's *Messiah*, scheduled a few weeks before Christmas. The Sunday afternoon of the performance was cold and blustery, the fresh snow blowing off the lake turning everything around Chicago into a Christmas card. Wheaton looked like a winter wonderland.

Billy, however, needed nothing at all to increase his sense of awe as he approached the women's dormitory for his date with Ruth. Days previously, he had already written to his mother, informing her that he had fallen in love. Nevertheless, he stood, mouth agape, when he greeted Ruth at the door. Even bundled in her heavy, red-plaid winter coat, Ruth still looked slender, her hazel eyes and radiant facial features highlighted even more by bright-red lipstick and a black velvet hat. As Billy gazed at her, she exuded a beauty that reminded him of a movie star.

When he finally caught his breath, he politely offered Ruth his arm to assist her on the snowy steps and sidewalk. "Why, thank you, Billy," Ruth said as she smiled and linked her arm around his.

They walked the short distance from Ruth's dorm to Pierce

Chapel, and Billy couldn't take his eyes off her. Once inside the chapel, designed as a worship center similar to a church with an altar area at the front, Billy helped Ruth remove her coat, and they settled into their seats. The singers and orchestra had meticulously practiced Handel's most famous piece of music, and the excitement onstage was palpable. But the excitement Billy sensed far surpassed even that.

The lights went down in the auditorium, and the music began; all the while, Billy's attention was on Ruth. He tried his best to sit back and enjoy the presentation, but his eyes kept wandering back to the beautiful woman beside him. Billy barely heard the music.

Ruth sensed Billy looking at her and occasionally hinted at a smile, but she maintained her gaze, looking straight ahead, keeping her attention steadfastly focused on the performance at the front of the chapel. Following an outstanding rendition of one of the better-known portions of the oratorio, Ruth looked over at Billy to see if he had enjoyed it. She found his eyes glued to her; he wasn't even paying attention to the music.

"The altar is up there, Billy. Not on my head," she said.

Billy blushed, and Ruth turned her gaze back toward the front . . . smiling.

The winter sky had already darkened by the time the performance concluded. The snow had stopped falling, and the air was brisk but not bone-chilling, so Billy and Ruth strolled across campus to the large Victorian home of Wheaton professor Mortimer B. Lane and his family for a cup of tea and some conversation. Billy had a thousand questions for Ruth, especially about her childhood and her upbringing in China.

"China is a beautiful but tragic country," Ruth told him. "Starvation, indescribable human suffering, the horrors of wars.

But I still want to go back. There is so much work to be done there."

Billy listened intently to Ruth's description of her former homeland, hanging on her every word, falling deeper and deeper for her as she spoke.

"I can get you a free Fuller brush," he gushed foolishly, his mind racing ahead, wondering what he could possibly give to her.

"Billy?" Ruth looked at him.

"Oh, it's horrible! The—the—the starvation! The horrors of war! Wait . . . is it China or Tibet? Never mind."

"Are you okay?" Ruth asked with a laugh.

"As a missionary?" Billy's mind was still racing into the future. "I mean you. Not me. I'm sorry, Ruth."

"Billy, I watched my father give up everything to serve the people of China. Sacrifice and love were the signature elements of his life. He gave everything to share the love of Jesus through his skills to heal them as a physician."

Billy grew quiet and contemplative, humbled by Ruth's assessment of her father's medical mission ministry and her own desires to serve God. He tried to speak, but the words got caught in his throat. Finally, he eked out, "Wow. That's a real sacrifice . . ."

"It's more than sacrifice," Ruth said. "It's commitment by choice. We lived in the aftermath of the Boxer Rebellion, which resulted in the now-famous China Martyrs." Ruth paused and looked deeply into Billy's eyes, wanting desperately for him to understand her heart. "Billy, 182 Protestant missionaries and 500 Christian Chinese gave their lives for the gospel. Voluntarily! And then, when things could not get any worse, foreign troops marched into China and avenged the deaths of the martyrs. Then 50,000 Chinese were summarily accused of being among the Boxers and

were killed. Hatred for hatred. Death for death. It was one of the
bloodiest clashes between Westerners and the Chinese. I have seen
things and known things that—" Ruth stopped abruptly, nearly
losing her composure as tears welled in her eyes.

Billy was stunned. "You're . . . you're crying, Ruth?"

Ruth looked into Billy's face and recognized a good-hearted,
sincere man. "The way I see it, Billy"—she spoke slowly, her eyes
never leaving his—"if you are not willing to live your life for something greater than yourself, well, then life is not really worth living."

Billy looked at her tenderly, his eyes plumbing the depths of
hers. Billy knew that he had never met anyone quite like Ruth Bell.

He spoke softly but passionately, "I believe . . . that is the most
profoundly beautiful set of words I have ever heard strung
together." He continued gazing into her eyes, catching a glimpse
of her heart, deeply moved as he repeated her words. "'If you are
not willing to live your life for something greater than yourself,
well, then life is not really worth living.'"

Ruth smiled and gently broke the somber, spiritual mood, but
not by much. "What about you?" she asked. "What is it you want
to do with your life?"

"Well, I say . . . what you say . . ." Billy fumbled awkwardly
with his words.

Ruth laughed sweetly. "What does that mean?"

"It means . . ." Billy paused to gain confidence in what he
wanted to say as he looked at Ruth. "It means I believe God is
calling me to preach the gospel."

Ruth looked intrigued. "Do you mean as an evangelist?"

Billy nodded slowly, unsure what her reaction might be.

"Then do it!" Ruth encouraged him. "And do it with all your
heart."

Billy smiled, strengthened by Ruth's support. "Really? I mean, that's okay by you?"

"Do you need my permission?" Ruth asked whimsically.

"I'd like it," Billy responded, more seriously than Ruth had expected.

She recognized that something very real was going on between them . . . and it nearly frightened her. She looked into Billy's blue eyes and spoke ever so quietly, "You have it."

In his youthful days, Billy Frank Graham might have kissed a young woman who looked as Ruth did at that moment. But this was no fickle puppy love. This was different. Totally different. Billy looked at Ruth tenderly, searching her eyes hopefully as he reached over and took hold of her hand. Ruth did not pull away.

After escorting Ruth back to her dorm and saying a reluctant good night, Billy walked slowly to his own dorm. He kicked at the snow, partly out of sheer elation at being with Ruth and partly out of frustration for not knowing how to relate to a woman like her. At long last he entered his room, where Howard, Grady, and George were laughing, talking, and goofing off while awaiting his triumphant return. They immediately grew silent.

"Hey, Romeo, how'd it go?" one of the guys finally asked.

Billy was lost in thought as he slowly took off his coat, and then looked up as though just noticing that the guys were in his room.

"Well, what gives?" Grady asked. "How was your—" Grady stopped short, noticing the dazed look on Billy's face. The guys' first thought was that Billy had fared no better than many other suitors who had hoped to court Ruth Bell.

But they were wrong.

Dreamy eyed, Billy leaned back against the wall, totally smitten by Ruth. "How can one person be so beautiful," Billy asked aloud the question that he had been pondering along the way home, "and be so spiritual at the same time?"

Howard, Grady, and George looked at one another and shrugged. "Oh no," Grady said with a smile, as he patted Billy on the shoulder. "You are in way deep, my boy."

About that same time, the moonlight peeking through Ruth's window bathed her dormitory room in a soft glow. Within her heart, Ruth was experiencing another sort of glowing warmth. Marjorie had already fallen asleep, so Ruth quietly changed into her nightgown and, as was her custom, knelt beside her bed to pray. "Dear Lord. I just met this man, and I thought I knew what my life's work would be and where it would take me. But if You let me serve You with that man," she prayed fervently, "I'd consider it the greatest privilege in my life."[1]

Ruth loved to express her inner thoughts through writing, so later she wrote a poem that poignantly described her feelings during that time:

Dear God, I prayed, all unafraid
(as we're inclined to do)
I do not need a handsome man
But let him be like You;
I do not need one big and strong nor yet so very tall,
Nor need he be some genius,
Or wealthy, Lord, at all;
But let his head be high, dear God,
And let his eye be clear,
His shoulders straight, whate'er his state,

---

1. Martin, *A Prophet with Honor*, 82.

Whate'er his earthly sphere;
And let his face have character,
A ruggedness of soul,
And let his whole life show, dear God,
A singleness of goal;
Then, when he comes,
(as he will come)
With quiet eyes aglow,
I'll understand that he's the man
I prayed for, long ago.[2]

❧

One of the advantages of attending a small Christian college was that the students got to see one another regularly, whether they wanted to or not. The danger, of course, was that when romances blossomed, especially between young men and women seriously seeking God's direction for their lives, it was all too easy to see them as a "couple" prematurely. Administrators, professors, local pastors, and even fellow students often cautioned students about getting "emotionally and spiritually involved" too quickly, but whirlwind romances sometimes resulted in ill-advised engagements and marriages nonetheless.

Billy was convinced after their first date that he and Ruth would be married. He even wrote home, telling his family that he planned to marry Ruth. Convincing Ruth of that, however, might take some time, as Billy soon discovered.

---

2. Betty Frist, *My Neighbors, the Billy Grahams* (Nashville, TN: Broadman Press, 1983), 3.

They saw each other regularly on Wheaton's campus and enjoyed long walks and conversations, even in the cool winter weather. One night they were sitting on a stone wall in front of one of Wheaton's dorms, when the conversation turned to Ruth's deep, lifelong commitment to be a missionary. "Since I was twelve, I've had my mind set on staying single so that I can be a missionary in Tibet," Ruth said. "I couldn't ask a husband, or children, to make the same sacrifice as me."

Billy appeared intent and concerned, as though searching for a response. Finally he asked, "Is there something wrong with being a wife and mother?"

"No, of course not," Ruth replied. "It's the most wonderful thing in the world—for some women. But not all."

Billy rose suddenly, his eyes to the ground. He turned to Ruth and out of the blue said, "I could go to Tibet."

Billy Graham pouring his life out as a missionary wasn't such an outlandish idea, actually. One of the reasons Billy had enrolled in Wheaton's anthropology program was the remote possibility that he might end up on a foreign mission field following his graduation. He knew he felt called to preach the gospel, and people in foreign nations needed to hear the good news as much as Americans. Maybe meeting Ruth, a woman with a heart for missionary work, was part of God's plan. Billy wasn't sure. The only thing he knew for sure was that he wanted to marry Ruth.

Later that night, Billy stood out in the hall of the men's dormitory, by his floor's lone pay phone, waiting patiently as the operator connected his collect call home. Soon his mother answered the call and accepted the charges.

After filling in his mother on the picayune details of his day, Billy got down to the matter most on his mind: Ruth. He described her in detail; he told of her dedication, her beauty, her vibrant sense of humor, her bright eyes, and her quick laugh that always made Billy smile.

"Billy, that's wonderful," Morrow Graham said, smiling on the other end of the line.

But Billy wasn't done yet. He continued extolling Ruth's virtues as he slid down to the floor and leaned his head back against the wall. "She's the most wonderful girl I've ever met. The most beautiful, the smartest, caring . . . she's so compassionate, Momma . . ."

"I'm so happy for you, Billy," Morrow said sincerely.

Just then Frank Graham passed by and saw his wife on the phone. Realizing that she was talking to Billy—and that he'd probably called collect—his father said, "Tell Billy hello—and tell him it's too expensive to stay on the phone this long."

Morrow nodded to Frank.

Meanwhile Billy gushed on about Ruth. "I wanna marry her, Momma," he said.

Surprised at the suddenness of it all, yet recognizing the sincerity in her son's voice, Morrow asked, "Are you sure, Billy? You're sure she's the one? I mean, *the* one?"

Billy didn't have to think twice before answering. He leaned his head back and spoke softly into the phone, "She's the one, Momma. There is no other."

Chapter Ten

As winter melted into springtime at Wheaton College, love was in the air. More than a few student couples announced their engagements as graduation loomed in the near future. Billy himself had a new lilt to his step, as his relationship with Ruth flourished. The smile that formed so easily on his lips seemed to be there perpetually. Billy was in love, or at least as much as he knew of it.

Much of their courtship took place in church, or at least in church services, as Billy had taken on the responsibilities as interim pastor of the United Gospel Tabernacle, a church that met on Sundays in the Masonic Lodge on Wesley Street in Wheaton. Dr. Edman, Wheaton's president, had preached at "The Tab," as it was known to Wheaton students and faculty who attended services there, when he was a history professor at the college, but when he became president in 1940, he gave up the pastorate, and the congregation filled the pulpit with "supply" preachers, or guest speakers. Billy had spoken at The Tab frequently, so no one was surprised when the congregation asked Billy to be their pastor, even though he was still a student at Wheaton.

Besides his full-time job preaching at The Tab, as well as occasional evangelistic speaking opportunities, Billy also worked as a mover with Johnny Streater to help pay his way through school. With studying, preaching, and moving furniture, little time was left for courting Ruth, so for "dates" she sometimes accompanied Billy to church services in which he was preaching. Other dates were with friends, playing games, canoeing on the Fox River about ten miles from Wheaton, or simply packing a picnic basket and enjoying an afternoon off campus at a park.

Even in their dates, Ruth revealed the spunk and strong will that would characterize their relationship. For instance, one beautiful afternoon, when she and Billy slipped away from campus for a picnic, Billy brought along a baseball and some mitts so he could show Ruth how to play catch.

They found an ideal spot, away from the crowds at the park, spread a blanket out on the ground, and placed their picnic basket on top of the blanket. "Okay, let's play catch before we eat," Billy enthused.

They separated by about fifty feet, both wearing their baseball fielder's gloves. "All right, now, Ruth," Billy cautioned before tossing. "Watch the ball. Don't let it hit you. It will hurt." He started to pitch the ball to Ruth overhand, but then, out of respect for her fragility, he paused and instead tossed the ball in a soft, underhand lob.

Ruth caught the ball easily and smacked it in her mitt.

"Good! Good!" Billy called. "Now, throw it back."

Before tossing the ball back to Billy, Ruth cocked her head

and raised her eyebrows as she offered the same advice. "All right, Billy. You keep your eye on the ball; don't let it hit you, because it will hurt."

Billy chuckled. "Okay, Ruth."

Ruth reared her arm back, and in her best sandlot baseball form, learned when she was a girl on the mission field in China, she whaled the ball to Billy.

Smack! The ball cracked into Billy's glove, and he winced in pain. "Wow. That's . . . uh . . . that's great," he said, shaking his hand behind his back so Ruth wouldn't notice. "Let's try another one." They tossed the ball back and forth a few more times, with Ruth zinging fastballs into Billy's mitt.

"Araaaah!" Billy blurted, as another of Ruth's full-speed pitches fired into his glove. Pulling his left hand out of the glove, he noticed that his palm was already turning red from Ruth's blistering throws. "Maybe we should go eat now," he called to her. Laughing, she ran to join him on the picnic blanket.

Each day, Billy looked for Ruth between classes to share even just a few moments with her. One day, as he was coming down the staircase—in the same stairwell where he and Ruth had met—Billy saw Ruth trudging wearily up the stairs, on her way to class. "Hey, where are you . . ." Billy started to say, but when he saw her face, he suddenly knew something was not right. With other students stepping past them on the stairs, Billy looked down from above her. "Ruth? What's wrong?" he asked.

Ruth gazed up at Billy sadly, then blinked back a tear and took a deep breath. "My sister has been diagnosed with tuberculosis. I have to leave school to care for her. I wanted to tell you myself . . . why I won't be seeing you again."

Billy couldn't believe his ears. He stood stunned on the staircase, looking into Ruth's distraught face. For a long moment, neither of them said a word as Ruth searched Billy's face, wondering how he might react to this news. After a few more seconds, she turned to leave, but Billy grabbed her arm. As other students crossed in front and behind them, Billy looked into Ruth's eyes. "Then marry me."

"What?" It was Ruth's turn to be stunned.

"Marry me, Ruth. We'll help her. We'll take care of her. Together."

"Oh, Billy. I can't," Ruth replied sadly. "Not now. Not yet. Maybe not ever. I don't know. Strange, isn't it? You think you know what you want, and all of a sudden life . . ."

"I just can't give up on you," Billy pleaded as he stepped down to the same step where Ruth stood.

Ruth looked at him lovingly, but she had no answers. There was nothing else to say. She fell into his arms, and they embraced on the staircase. It wasn't a hug between lovers, nor was it a hug between friends. It was the uniting of two kindred souls in a pure love and concern for each other. After a few moments, Billy felt Ruth gently pulling away, and he released her. As much as he hated to do it, he knew he had to let her go.

☙

In the middle of the second semester, Ruth left Wheaton to care for her sister, Rosa, who had been hospitalized in New Mexico. Billy had to admire Ruth's love for her sister and her willingness to forgo her own college education, but he was sad to see her go. Alone in his room, Billy bowed his head and prayed for Rosa's recovery as well as Ruth's safety. Most of all, he prayed that God would bring her back to him.

Meanwhile, Billy continued preaching as often as possible, practicing everywhere he went. Sometimes he'd walk to the outskirts of Wheaton and practice his preaching on a street corner, calling out to passersby, sharing verses of Scripture with people as they walked by him. Most of his hearers tried to avoid him. Billy tried his best to win people over, but with little effectiveness.

"No matter what you may have done, the Lord watches over you," he called out to a man going by on the street. "The Lord watches and cares for you . . ." Billy called after him as the man continued on his way, paying no attention whatsoever to Billy's preaching.

In a shadowy alley, leaning up against the side of a gray stone building, a disheveled black man listened to Billy with disdain. The man had been living on the streets since the Depression; he'd seen Billy's kind before and had heard all of the well-intentioned but impotent words the uptown preachers had to offer. The sophisticated clergymen sometimes came to the alley, offering a few morsels of food and a plethora of grandiose words. But then they were gone, back to their comfortable neighborhoods, having made no lasting impact.

"I don't see no Lord watching over me, kid," the homeless man called out to Billy. "The Lord wants nothing to do with me. See the way people walks away from me? Nobody wants me, preacher."

Billy walked slowly into the shadows and looked at the homeless black man. Although Billy never exhibited the least racial bigotry, many white Christians in the South would have nothing to do with the "Negroes." Black people were not permitted in the predominantly white churches any more than they were in the white schools, restaurants, or on public buses. They were considered second-class citizens. Billy knew that when he stepped into the shadows.

"That's not true, sir," he said respectfully to the black man on the ground.

"If you want money for your preachin', you done come to the wrong place," the disheveled man said.

Hurt momentarily creased Billy's face as he realized that this poor homeless man harbored many of the same misgivings about preachers that he himself once held. "I didn't come here for money," Billy said straightforwardly.

"What did ya come here for?"

It was a good question, one that Billy had already been asking himself. Yet when it was posed by the helpless man in the shadows, Billy suddenly knew the correct answer. "I came to do the Lord's work," Billy answered.

The man got up off the ground and moved menacingly in Billy's direction. "Shouldn't you be in your pajamas?" he sneered derisively. "Tucked into bed with your teddy bear? Drinkin' a glass o' milk?"

Billy ignored the man's taunts; he didn't back off; instead, he stepped closer to the man and spoke to him kindly but boldly. "You can't be found unless you are first lost, sir. The Lord can find you and fix you, if you let Him. Put your trust in Jesus. He can give your life back again. Take Him into your heart."

For a moment, Billy thought the man might attack him, but he didn't. Instead, he lowered his head and began to sob, softly at first, then more profusely.

Instinctively, Billy moved forward and placed his hand on the down-and-out man's shoulder.

"Help me," the man begged through his tears. "Can you help me, preacher?"

"What is your name, sir?" Billy asked.

"Darryl," he replied, and then to Billy's surprise, the man fell on Billy's shoulder, weeping uncontrollably. "My name's Darryl," he sobbed.

Without thinking of what other people might say, Billy immediately reached around the sobbing man and embraced him tightly. With his white cheek pressed against Darryl's black one, Billy began to pray. "Father God, Darryl and I come to You today. And I don't believe this is an accident. I believe You had this planned for us, two thousand years before Darryl and I were born. I believe that. *I believe.*"

Although Darryl's life was changed that day, he could not have imagined that this moment was as significant for Billy as it was for him. Heaven would be more heavily populated as a result.

☙

In New Mexico, Ruth Bell sat in a rocker, reading to her sister, Rosa, as she had done each evening since arriving at her bedside. Though Rosa had been discharged from the hospital, her body remained weak. By early July, she was still a long way from regaining her strength, and the doctors estimated that it could take another six months before she was back to her normal health. So Ruth prepared her meals, changed her bedding, washed her clothing, and did anything else that Rosa could not do for herself. Since both young women were readers, they tried to spend part of each day with a book, and Rosa enjoyed drifting off to sleep each evening to the sound of Ruth's voice reading the Scripture or some classic story.

When she was certain that Rosa was sleeping soundly, Ruth slipped downstairs and sat at the kitchen table to catch up on her own correspondence.

On this night, Ruth was writing a very special letter, addressed to Billy. As she wrote, she poured out her heart to him, the original note turning into a thick letter that barely fit in the envelope. As Ruth prepared to seal the envelope, she paused, bowed her head, and prayed over the letter, asking God to bless it and to cause Billy to receive it in the right way. She then sealed the letter with a sense of utter joy, excitement, and freedom.

The letter arrived at the Wheaton College post office a few days later, and Billy found it waiting for him when he went to pick up his mail after morning classes. He received several pieces of mail that day—a rare treat for a college student—but rather than standing in front of the bronze mailboxes and reading his mail, as some students did, Billy scooped up the letters and headed back to his dorm.

Sitting on his bed, he quickly tore open the envelope bearing the New Mexico return address. He didn't have to read far before he found what he was looking for. Slowly, the full impact of Ruth's neatly written words dawned on him. He gulped hard, holding the letter tightly, as though it might flutter away if he failed to grasp it just so. He read the words again. "She said yes," he said aloud. Suddenly, overcome with emotion and adrenaline, Billy bolted off the bed.

"Yes. Yes! She said *yes!*" Billy shouted as he headed for the door, with no particular destination in mind, waving the letter as he went.

In the hallway, a group of male students was standing around, shooting the breeze, as Billy burst out of his room, shouting and sharing his jubilation with anyone who would listen. "She said yes!" he shouted and waved the letter for all to see as he made his way down the corridor.

A few doors down, Billy spied Grady and called out to him, "Grady! She said yes!"

"What are you talkin about, Billy?" Grady asked with a laugh, totally in the dark as to the reason for Billy's elation. Yet caught up in the moment, he couldn't help sharing Billy's ebullience.

"Ruth," Billy exclaimed. "She said yes, Grady. Yes! She wants to marry me!"

Grady could hardly believe his ears. Ruth Bell, campus prize, wanting to marry Billy? "I hope you got it in writing," he said with a chortle.

"I do," Billy said. "Right here! It's right here in her *own handwriting*. Look!" Billy began reading Ruth's long letter to Grady, as Grady kept moving toward the exit stairwell, trying to get to class.

Billy read aloud above the din in the hallway, "'Billy, it would be the greatest honor to be your wife.'" He looked at Grady. "She wrote that, Grady."

"Congrats, ole man," Grady said as he edged closer to the doorway, still laughing along with the other guys at Billy's exuberance. "You were able to do what no other man on campus could do."

Billy didn't even notice Grady slip out the door. He was in his own world as he leaned his back against the wall. "She said yes," he told himself again. Then, with an ethereal expression on his face, his eyes looking off into the future, Billy held up Ruth's letter, smiled, and in a dreamy voice softly said, "Ahh, Mr. and Mrs. Ruth Graham."

⌘

Although Billy and Ruth became engaged in early July 1941, they didn't marry until two years later, in August 1943, after they had both graduated from Wheaton College. At several junctures, there was some question whether they would marry at all!

For one thing, Ruth sometimes questioned whether Billy was genuinely serious about his willingness to go to China as a missionary, and Billy himself grappled with that same question. At one point after Ruth's return to Wheaton, she had such serious doubts about Billy being called to the mission field that she suggested they break off their engagement and not see each other for a while. Billy continued to assuage her concerns, and they got their relationship back on track, albeit with a full understanding that they would not marry until after both of them had graduated.

When the Japanese bombed Pearl Harbor on December 7, 1941, Billy immediately contacted the War Department, volunteering to be an army chaplain. As an ordained Baptist minister, he felt certain there would be a place for him in the Chaplain Corps. "Finish your education first, and get a bit of experience. Then we'll talk," the military told him.

The war further threw Ruth's intention of returning to Tibet as a missionary into somewhat of a fog. Her parents had returned home from China prior to Pearl Harbor, but when the Japanese moved into mainland China, the Bells' ministry there had to be curtailed as well.

By the winter of 1943, with only one more semester of college to complete, Billy began to think seriously about how he might support Ruth as his wife. Bob Van Kampen, a young executive with the Gideon Association, the group that places Bibles in hotel rooms,

informed Billy about the possibility of becoming the pastor of the
Village Church, a Baptist church in Western Springs, about twenty
miles southeast of Wheaton. Billy jumped at the chance, accepting
the position without even consulting Ruth, his bride-to-be.

When Ruth found out about Billy's decision, she was angry
and hurt. She couldn't believe that Billy would be so insensitive as
to not even seek her opinion or advice in a matter that clearly had
ramifications for both of them. With no lack of spunk, Ruth let
him know it!

Ruth knew, of course, that Billy had few aspirations to become
a full-time career pastor, so both she and Billy regarded the position at the struggling little church as a temporary step: Billy saw it
as preparation to become an army chaplain, and Ruth saw it as
preparation for their future work together on the mission field,
where she still hoped they'd be going, "as soon as we can."

Surviving such tensions, Ruth and Billy were married the
evening of Friday, August 13, 1943, in Gaither Chapel on the
Presbyterian conference grounds at Montreat, North Carolina, a
short drive from Asheville. Billy's mentor from Florida Bible
Institute, Dr. John Minder, conducted the wedding ceremony,
assisted by Dr. Kerr Taylor, a former missionary to China and a
close friend of the Bell family. Special music was sung by Andrew
Yang, from Chinkiang, China. As Billy and Ruth said, "I do" that
evening, few people attending the ceremony had any doubts that
the couple would one day serve as missionaries in China.

After a brief honeymoon in North Carolina, Billy and Ruth
headed back to Hinsdale, Illinois, to set up housekeeping and to
serve the parishioners at the Western Springs church. The congregation of fewer than one hundred members had constructed a new
facility, but they had run out of money after completing only the

basement. The only windows in the building were at ground level, so they provided little light and even less of a view. With her "high church" Presbyterian background, Ruth referred to the building as "junky" and said, "I feel like we are having church in an air-raid shelter!" But the congregation was kind to the young couple, and the experience at Western Springs prepared them for a much larger area of influence.

It was also while Billy and Ruth were serving at Western Springs that Billy met a man who was going to change his life.

Chapter Eleven

Amazingly, at eighty-three years of age and fighting dementia, Charles Templeton could still spin a good story. Even the jaded television crew members, who had seen and heard it all, were listening intently as Templeton told of Billy and Ruth Graham's romance. Deborah Matthews, however, was growing more anxious by the minute. Touched as she was by the sweetness and innocence of Billy and Ruth's relationship—reminding Deborah of her own true love, three husbands ago—Deborah recognized that her career was on the line if she didn't find some tantalizing tidbits to discredit Billy Graham's integrity and lifelong ministry. She was equally intrigued by the man who "could have been" Graham, so she posed a pointed question to Templeton, hoping to appeal to his pride.

"So what you're saying, then, is that despite your great abilities and Billy Graham's mediocrity, he seemed almost destined for greatness?"

Templeton eyed the reporter suspiciously. He was not about to succumb to her verbal traps, but she was onto something when she mentioned Billy's ordinariness. "It's fascinating, actually," Templeton said, shifting slightly in his bed. "Billy's life plan at this point was nothing more than to be a pastor in a little church, go into the army as a second lieutenant, become a chaplain, get shipped overseas, and then, provided he lived through the horrors of war, he would become a missionary with Ruth, probably in China."

Templeton chuckled. "Billy didn't know the difference between Tibet and China. Ha! End of story. There's no greatness there! I'm telling you, young lady, at each stage of Billy's life, left to his own devices, Billy would have taken the path that led to mediocrity. But something always stepped in to save him.

"I, on the other hand . . . I was focused; I had goals! I saw myself preaching in front of twenty-five, thirty thousand, forty thousand people. And I did it! Billy? If it was left up to Billy, he would have been content to be your local pastor. Nothing more."

Templeton again swatted at his invisible visitors. "Stay away. *Stay away!*" he shouted.

Deborah turned to her cameraman. "Are you getting this?" she whispered.

"Got it," he replied.

Matthews smiled. "Now we are getting somewhere," she said to herself.

෴

WESTERN SPRINGS CHURCH, SPRING 1944

Billy and Ruth sat in the kitchen of their four-room, furnished apartment, the upstairs of their landlady's home at 214 South Clay

Street. The radio played in the background as Billy studied his Bible and Ruth thumbed through a magazine, diligently searching for ideas Billy could use in his sermons.

"This would make a good illustration." She pointed at a story in a major newsmagazine as she handed the magazine to Billy.

Billy scanned the article, nodding and affirming. He smiled at Ruth and said, "I like it. Thanks, Ruth." Laying the magazine next to his Bible, he began to read the entire article.

Behind them, the music swelled, and a voice on the radio said, "This is Torrey Johnson, coming to you from *Songs in the Night,* saying, have a pleasant day, and may the good Lord always shine down on you."

Just then, the telephone rang, and Ruth picked up the receiver. "Hello. Pastor Graham's residence," she said kindly.

Billy looked over at Ruth, wondering if there was an emergency among the parishioners. Ruth saw the inquiring look on his face and waved him off. As she listened further, however, a look of amazement spread across her own face.

"Mr. Johnson? Yes. Of course we know you," she said excitedly. "Yes . . . Yes. This is Ruth. His wife . . . Yes. He is! He's right here, sir." Ruth handed the telephone to Billy, as she mouthed the name of the caller: *Torrey Johnson!*

Billy leaped up and took the receiver from her hand. "Hello?" he said tentatively. "Naw! . . . Really?" Billy looked at the radio, from which he'd just heard Johnson's voice a few moments ago. He held the phone out and looked at it, then back at the radio, and then quickly put the phone back to his ear.

"Mr. Johnson?" Billy glanced at the radio again. "How'd you do that so fast? Er, never mind. Well, goodness gracious!"

Billy had actually met Torrey Johnson ever so briefly one

afternoon as he was driving down the street near Western Springs church. A man driving in the opposite direction pulled up to him. "Are you Billy Graham?" the man had asked.

"Yes, sir. Yes, I am," Billy had replied, thinking the man needed something from the church, or perhaps some spiritual guidance.

"I'm Torrey Johnson."

"Oh, yes, sir!" Billy responded. "I've heard you on the radio."

"I'd like to talk with you sometime."

"Yes, sir. Anytime at all."

"Okay, fine. I'll give you a call."

And now Torrey Johnson, a leading Chicago clergyman, was on the phone talking with Billy. Torrey got right to the point. "Billy, as you may know, I'm a pastor of a large, growing church, and I have too many things going on right now. In addition to my church responsibilities, I have two radio shows, my main program on Sunday afternoon, and another program called *Songs in the Night*. I was wondering if you would be willing to take over that program. I'd like to give it to you; I think you could do a good job on it. You've heard the program, right?"

Torrey Johnson's *Songs in the Night* aired on WCFL in Chicago, one of the most powerful AM radio stations in the nation at that time. The station could be heard all over the Midwest, and on clear nights, as far away as the East Coast and much of the South. It was a tremendous opportunity, but it also cost a whopping $150 per week for the radio time. Billy took the matter to his church board, which initially rejected the idea due to the cost. But when Bob Van Kampen agreed to finance the program, Billy took it on. He invited a quartet from Wheaton College to sing a few songs on the program, and he preached and played emcee, all live for forty-five minutes.

Before long, Billy's voice was being broadcast across the nation. Ruth loved to sit at the kitchen table in the evenings, listening to him on WCFL. "This is Billy Graham, coming to you from *Songs in the Night*," his clear voice rang out. Sometimes Billy would even sit down with her, and they'd listen to the program together, thinking up ideas for new radio messages and gently critiquing the show as it stood. From the beginning, they both knew that the program needed something extra, something that would add a bit more interest than simply another preacher on the radio.

One evening, after Ruth and Billy came in from tossing a baseball outside, they were sitting in the living room, listening to WMBI, the radio outreach of Moody Bible Institute, when they heard a powerful baritone voice just finishing a song. When the music stopped, the singer said, "This is George Beverly Shea, for WMBI, wishing you and yours a good night."

"I need someone like him for *Songs in the Night*," Billy said nonchalantly to Ruth.

Ruth picked up on the idea immediately. "Why not *him*?" Ruth asked. "He's the best baritone in the country. Where is he?"

Billy looked at Ruth, as if inspired and at the same time amazed by her.

"George Beverly Shea? He's the staff announcer for Moody Bible Institute in Chicago. But why would he agree to be on my little radio show?"

"Maybe you just need to get your foot in the door, Mr. Fuller Brush salesman," Ruth said with a smile.

ᘒ

Driving alone on the open highway, dressed in one of his best suits and a pair of freshly shined shoes, Billy passed a familiar sign: Chicago. In his typical bold fashion, he was headed to WMBI radio station to track down George Beverly Shea. The singer-broadcaster was well-known in the Chicago area. Originally from Winchester, Ontario, Shea was one of eight children born to a Wesleyan Church pastor and his wife. He briefly attended Houghton College, in upstate New York, but was forced to drop out when his family ran into financial difficulties. He declined secular singing opportunities, choosing instead to sing only gospel songs. At the same time, he pursued a career in radio, first in New York and then in Chicago, where he had become a familiar voice by the early 1940s.

The WMBI radio station offices were located on the top floor of Moody's main building in downtown Chicago. Billy parked his car, made his way upstairs, and burst into the WMBI offices like a man on a mission.

A stoic, stodgy-looking secretary was seated at a large desk in the reception area. She looked surprised to see the unexpected visitor, and not particularly happy about it either. "May I help you, sir?" she asked perfunctorily, suspiciously eyeing the sharply dressed man in front of her.

"I'm here to see Mr. Shea," Billy said, as though George Beverly Shea and he were best friends.

The secretary wasn't buying that for a moment. She opened her appointment book and scanned the pages. "I don't see any appointments for him at this hour," she said protectively and with a bit of an accusatory tone to her voice.

Billy leaned over her desk. "I drove all the way up here from Western Springs just to see him," he implored.

"I see," she said. The secretary drew back slightly so she could better size up the tall, thin man with such a desperate look on his face. She knew that part of her job was to be the "keeper of the gate," the first line of defense against unwanted visitors who would waste her boss's time. She made a decision on the spot. "I'm sorry, sir, but he's busy. Would you like to make a proper appointment?" she asked stuffily, as though such an appointment would be very difficult for someone like Billy to obtain.

Just then, Billy looked to his right and saw George Beverly Shea's silhouette through the frosted window on the door to his inner office. Billy instantly recognized the handsome singer and could see that Shea was talking on the telephone at a desk. He appeared to be alone in the office. At that moment, Shea hung up the phone and rose from his chair, as though he were getting ready to leave. Billy did not want to waste the trip, and more important, he believed that he needed a marquee name such as George Beverly Shea on *Songs in the Night*, so he made an on-the-spot decision as well.

Billy looked back at the secretary behind the desk. "How about right now?" he said as he started for Shea's office door.

Frazzled and disturbed at such an intrusion, the secretary called out to Billy, "Sir! Sir, please!"

Just then Shea opened his door, and in his best Fuller Brush form, Billy slid his foot inside the doorway so the door couldn't be closed. He extended his hand to shake as the surprised singer was taken aback.

"Sir! You can't go in there!" the distraught secretary called out to no avail.

But Billy ignored the secretary's plaintive protests. "Mr. Shea," he said, grabbing Shea's hand and shaking it vigorously. "If I could just have a moment of your time, I believe I have an opportunity in which you might be interested."

Stunned but intrigued, immaculately dressed in a distinguished-looking suit and tie, Shea was surprised at the audacity of his enthusiastic visitor, but not upset. "All right," he replied. "Let's hear it."

Billy launched into his spiel, just as he had so many times before as a Fuller Brush salesman. "My name is Billy Graham, and . . ." Billy stopped cold and looked into Shea's eyes. "To be honest, sir, you could change *my* life."

Shea raised his eyebrows in a noncommittal but obviously interested expression. He motioned Billy inside his office. "Come on in," he said, closing the door behind them. The door had barely closed when Billy rapidly began laying out his plans to Shea, his arms flying in every direction as he spoke. "Mr. Shea, I'm sorry to intrude, but I just have a quick proposal for you to consider." And then Billy was off again, explaining in rapid-fire sentences how he had taken over Torrey Johnson's radio program on WCFL, and how it was such a great opportunity to reach people with the gospel, if he just had a featured soloist.

Outside in the reception area, the secretary sulked, frustrated that she was unable to hear the men speaking, even though she could see Shea shaking his head, appearing uncertain. Billy plowed on, exploding into animated enthusiasm, his dramatic, silhouetted hand gestures clearly visible behind the frosted window.

When Billy finally slowed down, he started over afresh. "Mr. Shea, my name is Billy Graham, and I'm the pastor at the Village Church in Western Springs," he said.

Shea nodded. "I've heard of you."

"Torrey Johnson has asked me to take over his radio program, and I'm convinced that it would be most successful if you'd agree to appear on it . . . on a regular basis."

"Well, I don't know," Shea hedged. "I'm rather busy . . ."

Billy kept right on, explaining how he saw the forty-five minute program working. Finally, for some reason—if nothing more
than the realization that he was not going to get rid of Billy otherwise—George Beverly Shea agreed to appear with Billy on *Songs
in the Night*. Neither man could have dreamed at the time that
their partnership would be perpetual, and they'd be working
together around the world for the next sixty years.

When Billy took over the program from Torrey Johnson, the
format had been about two- or three-minute-long vignettes, followed by a song, then more topical vignettes, followed by more
music, filling the entire forty-five minutes. At first, Billy followed
that pattern too, but in early December, he and George Beverly
Shea made a drastic change, deciding to broadcast live from the
Village Church, with an audience. The show took on an entirely
new energy as Shea sang and Billy preached. Adding to the excitement, WMBI signed on to broadcast the regular Sunday morning
services, live from the Western Springs church. Over the next few
months, scores of people attended the church simply to witness
and participate in the radio program.

Despite the changes, however, the program never lost its evangelistic thrust. As Ruth sat on the front row of the packed church,
thrilled with the response, "Bev" Shea sang in the background as
Billy addressed both the live audience and the radio audience.
"For many of you, the late night is the hardest time. You are alone
with your thoughts. The clutter of the day has ebbed away, and
the worries of life have settled in. Tonight, George Beverly Shea
and I will bring you a message and song of hope to help you make
it through the night. This is Billy Graham and George Beverly
Shea for *Songs in the Night*."

The program was a great success, drawing not only many new faces to the Village Church but also numerous invitations for Billy Graham to speak in various towns around the country where the radio program reached. Billy tried to accept as many of the speaking engagements as he could, sometimes causing tension with his own congregation because of his frequent absences. It wasn't a surprise to the local church leaders that Billy was being invited to preach in other places—even the church letterhead listed him as "pastor-evangelist"—but the frequency of his extended ministry disturbed some of the leadership who preferred more of a "stay at home" pastor. But from Billy's perspective, he was beginning to see the world as restless, searching for something that could bring peace with God after experiencing the horrors of World War II. His passion for evangelism expanded exponentially when he received a second call from Torrey Johnson, asking to meet with Billy about another ministry he had in mind.

 So

CHICAGO, 1944

Torrey Johnson knew he was not the world's greatest preacher, but the man had a gift for putting the right people together in the right place. His personality combined a bit of businessman, Vaudeville showman, and carnival barker with a passionate heart to see people's lives changed by putting their faith in God. He recognized that with the war winding down, a number of soldiers were returning home, their minds filled with images of death and their hearts hungry for something real and lasting—something that could not be blown away by man's inhumanity. And of course, many of the young men and women who had been away from home for so long were show-ing up on Chicago's busy Michigan Avenue, looking for some action to soothe their hearts, minds, and souls. Torrey decided that this was a prime opportunity to present young people with the gos-pel message of truth, love, and forgiveness.

He headed a committee to start what he called Chicagoland Youth for Christ, and his plan was to provide an upbeat "show" that would attract the flood of servicemen and women who hit the streets on Saturday nights by featuring a fast-paced variety of youth-oriented music—musicians of every sort, soloists, trios, quartets, instrumentalists, as well as dramatic presentations, and then present the crowd with a solid evangelistic message. That's where Billy came in.

Billy and Ruth sat opposite Torrey in his office as the Chicago preacher described his grandiose idea. "Billy, Ruth, I'm putting together a new outreach called Youth for Christ. I want someone who can preach the gospel and invite people to Christ. Not a sea-soned pro. An up-and-comer. I want someone whose career I can foster and grow and watch blossom. Who I want . . . is you, Billy Graham."

Billy's jaw dropped, and he sat momentarily speechless. "Me? I don't know what to say."

Ruth smiled. "The Lord speaks in strange ways."

"I guess so," Billy agreed, although still uncertain about Torrey's plan. Torrey, however, was already putting it all together in his mind—and he was thinking big—arena-sized big.

"You're going to need a team," Torrey instructed. "Have you got one? I'm talking about some good people around you, some musicians, a good soloist. Some people who can help you."

Billy thought for a moment, leaning forward, his chin in his hands. "I have T. W. and Grady Wilson. They are good men, men I've known since high school."

"And he's got George Shea," Ruth reminded them.

"That's great," Torrey responded. He thought for a moment as well, then said, "I'm going to put Chuck up there with you."

"Chuck?"

"Yes, Chuck Templeton," Torrey said, as though the idea somehow had just taken shape in his mind, and he could see all the details coming together.

Billy was awestruck. "Chuck . . . Charles Templeton?" he asked.

"That's right," Torrey replied.

"But . . . I'm just a small-town preacher, Torrey. Charles Templeton is big-time!"

∞

TEMPLETON'S HOSPITAL ROOM, 2001

"Charles Templeton is big-time!" The aged man repeated the words to be sure Deborah Matthews caught them. "Indeed!" he said. "Do you think anyone would have turned up to see Billy Graham? He couldn't fill a pup tent, let alone a circus tent or an arena. No, they came to see me! I was the juice! I spoke; they listened, enraptured! I held them in the palm of my hand and closed my fingers around them and would not let them go until I led them to Jesus." Templeton held out his hand as though inviting Deborah to Jesus. She stared at it awkwardly for a moment, when suddenly the cameraman interrupted.

"Battery's dead," he said in a hushed tone.

Deborah whirled around in her chair. *"WHAT?"*

Templeton continued right on with his story, oblivious to the drama unfolding in his room.

"Funny thing about Billy, though . . . we became friends. Best of friends . . ."

Deborah Matthews saw her career flash before her eyes. "Fix it!" she whispered hoarsely to the cameraman.

"I'm on it," he replied.

Deborah turned back to Templeton and smiled a fake smile, as though to reassure him that everything was all right. She needn't have bothered. He was unconcerned about a battery; his mind was on events that took place more than fifty years earlier.

Chapter Twelve

CHICAGO, ORCHESTRA HALL, 1944

Many of Torrey Johnson's friends and supporters opposed the suggestion of Billy preaching the first Youth for Christ services. After all, they had contracted Chicago's three-thousand-seat, internationally known Orchestra Hall for the initial event. They were concerned that the upstart Billy Graham, despite his newfound familiarity as a radio preacher, could not command a crowd large enough to fill the auditorium. If he did, he may not know what to do with such a crowd. The naysayers encouraged Torrey to look elsewhere for his keynote preacher. Many well-known speakers were traveling the country; if the services of the great Charles Templeton could not be secured for the first event, surely somebody was available who was better known than Billy Graham—anybody!

But Torrey was adamant; he wanted Billy for the first night. Whether it was a budget issue or a faith issue only Torrey could say, and he never did. He was interested in only one thing—somebody to present a clear-cut salvation message to the people of Chicago. He felt sure Billy Graham could do that.

On May 27, 1944, Orchestra Hall in Chicago was nearly full, packed with young men and women, many still wearing their military uniforms. Billy took one look at the crowd—the largest he'd ever seen before—and suddenly contracted a strong case of stage fright. But it was too late. Torrey was introducing him. "This is his first time speaking here in Chicago. Please welcome warmly an up-and-coming young evangelist, Billy Graham!"

The crowd responded kindly, although with no more enthusiasm than they would for any other virtually unknown person. Billy didn't mind. He breathed a final, quick prayer and strode onto the stage, his long legs crossing the platform in huge chunks.

"Thank you for making this country boy feel so welcome in the big city of Chicago," he began. The crowd broke into cheers, and almost instantly, Billy's stage fright dissipated. "The weather outside may be cold, but you have made this Southerner feel real warm at heart. Thank you. Now, I'm here to tell you . . ." He cracked a short joke and then plunged right into his sermon. As he did, he sensed an enormous freedom, as if a power far greater than his own was guiding his words. He spoke exuberantly and passionately, and at the close, he extended an invitation for those who wished to accept salvation through Jesus Christ to step forward to the front of the auditorium. At least forty young men and women did so. Both Torrey and Billy were elated.

Torrey immediately scheduled other Saturday night Youth for Christ events in Indianapolis, Philadelphia, and Detroit for later that year. Billy preached at all of them. When he found it no longer possible to juggle his responsibilities as the pastor of the Village Church in Western Springs, he had to make a decision. He chose to resign to enter full-time into evangelism, a calling he felt more profoundly than ever. Ruth, aware of the fact that returning to China would be a distant dream, told Billy that she realized their marriage was going to be one filled with good-byes. She was nonetheless excited about the possibility of Billy leading more young people into a relationship with Christ.

They almost faced saying good-bye for a much longer period of time when, in the summer of 1944, they received the news that Billy's application to be a military chaplain had finally been accepted. He was to report for a physical exam and induction into the army, and then to attend chaplain's classes at Harvard Divinity School in Boston before shipping out for the front. When Billy drove to Chicago for his military physical, he was pronounced "underweight." The army extended him a few months' time to fatten up before reporting for duty.

By September, he was ready to go, but then he came down with what he thought was a toothache. Before long, his entire throat and face were throbbing in pain. The doctor's diagnosis shocked both Billy and Ruth: at age twenty-six, Billy had developed an acute case of mumps on both sides of his face.

The daughter of a doctor, Ruth thought Billy's ailment was hilarious. Although she felt sorry for him and put him to bed just as the doctor instructed, she could hardly keep from laughing every time she explained to someone—including the army—that her husband had the mumps.

When the soreness in Billy's throat refused to go away after several weeks, however, neither Ruth or Billy found much humor in his condition. The fever intensified rather than dissipated, and the doctor's suggested two *weeks* in bed turned into two *months* of a dangerous, debilitating disease known as orchitis, which can cause sterility in men. The physical weakness resulting from the disease made Billy ineligible for overseas military service, and with the war turning in the Allies' favor, his service was not deemed necessary. He was relieved of his military commitment.

It was nearly Christmas by the time Billy was able to be up and around again, and although he was thrilled to be out of bed, his doctor gave him an extremely negative report. "Because of the orchitis, you and your wife will probably never be able to naturally conceive children." Ruth and Billy were devastated by the news, but they were nonetheless glad that he was alive and well. "Besides," they agreed, "children are a gift from the Lord, and if God wants us to have a child, He can overrule the prognosis of the doctors."

℘

The Youth for Christ events, or "rallies," as Torrey liked to call them, were so successful that in the spring of 1945, with World War II grinding to an end, Torrey thought they could take the Chicagoland Youth for Christ banner to Chicago Stadium, the vast sports arena. In addition to the usual array of talented young music artists, he recruited a one-thousand-voice choir to sing, filling the arena behind the speakers' platform. To bolster the event's appeal, Torrey booked the famous Chuck Templeton on the speakers' roster, along with Billy and several celebrity sports figures, military heroes, magicians, and others. The whole event took on the tone of a Broadway show or a Las Vegas extravaganza. For all its theatrics, the goal remained the same: to see young men and women converted or renewed in their relationships with Jesus Christ.

The mood in Chicago Stadium was ebullient as nearly twenty

thousand young people filled the arena. Templeton took the stage first, while a fresh-faced quartet dressed to the nines, waving the Chicagoland Youth for Christ banner, stood behind him. Holding forth in the spotlight, Chuck Templeton addressed the gathering with skill and dynamic verbal prowess, wowing the crowd with his brilliant elocution and penetrating insights. His speaking style was not so much the Mordecai Ham brand of hellfire and condemnation as it was a persuasive sales pitch, logically laying out the reasons why any young person could live better by entrusting his or her life to God.

"I'm here to tell you that God is real!" Templeton told the crowd as he brought his message to a close. "He is the answer to the perplexing questions of life. He is not only the author of this thing we call faith, but He is the one who can complete it in your life, tonight. Put your faith in Him. He will not disappoint the trusting heart!"

As Chuck Templeton concluded his talk, the audience erupted exuberantly, instinctively rising to its feet in a standing ovation. Sitting on the front row, Ruth Graham rose as well, smiling and applauding, yet somewhat reserved, almost as if something about Chuck Templeton's performance troubled her, but she couldn't quite put her finger on it. Shaking her head, she joined in with the jubilant crowd. Besides, Cliff Barrows, a talented young song leader, had stepped onto the stage and was leading the audience in a song with a bouncing, lilting melody. "Nothing is impossible, when you put your trust in God . . ."

Backstage, a crowd of handlers surrounded Chuck Templeton, helping him off the stage as Torrey's professional stage crew scurried about, moving cables, bringing up lights, preparing the stage for the next "act." Behind the flurry, the Graham team—Grady, T. W., and

Billy—stared in wide-eyed awe at the swirl of activity. Suddenly all three of them felt strangely out of place. T. W. straightened his tie, and Grady, a stocky fellow anyhow, tugged on the legs of what Billy jokingly referred to as Grady's "flood pants."

Although Billy had spoken at other Youth for Christ events, he had never seen anything like this. He stood offstage, wearing a New York Yankees baseball cap, in awe of Charles Templeton's performance and his confident persona as Templeton made his way toward the exit.

"Dear Lord, help me," Billy prayed quietly, his knees knocking as the crowd out front roared in laughter at something going on center stage. Billy began pacing back and forth, simply to keep his knees from banging together.

Chuck Templeton saw Billy pacing and veered in his direction. Just then, Torrey Johnson approached from the opposite direction, the two men meeting just behind Billy. "Great job, Chuck!" Torrey gushed. "Just the right touch."

Billy looked up anxiously from where he was silently praying, uncertain whether his lips were forming words or simply quivering. When he saw Torrey and Templeton nearby, he quickly removed his baseball cap and attempted to flatten his hair with his hand.

Torrey approached Billy with an arm around Chuck's shoulders. "Chuck Templeton, Billy Graham. Billy, this is Chuck Templeton." Torrey slapped both men on the back. "You guys have a lot in common."

"I can't tell you what a pleasure and an honor it is to meet you, Reverend Templeton," Billy said politely, as he and Templeton shook hands warmly.

"Chuck," Templeton said. "Nobody ever calls me Reverend Templeton. And I'm glad of that. My pleasure to meet you, Billy."

Templeton nodded toward the Yankees cap. "Is that your 'good luck' hat?"

"Yeah, I think I'm going to need an awful lot more than luck tonight. I've never seen so many people in one place in my life."

"You'll do fine," Templeton said with a laugh. "They're quite a friendly bunch."

"I sure hope so," Billy said, nodding his head.

Templeton was struck by Billy's down-to-earth, unpretentious attitude and liked him immediately. He decided to stick around and listen to what the new guy had to say. "Better hurry," he said, patting Billy on the back as they heard the emcee's voice starting the introduction.

"All the way from the little-bitty town of Western Springs, please welcome Billy Graham!"

Billy looked back at Charles Templeton. "Pray for me, Chuck. I'm scared to death. This is the big leagues, and I've never been here."

"Think of it like this, Billy. You've already hit the home run." He paused as the audience's applause filled the arena. "All you have to do now is round the bases."

Billy nodded, tossed his baseball cap to T. W., and stepped out into the spotlight. He quickly took command of the microphone, starting slowly, building to a crescendo, betraying none of his fear. Watching from backstage, Chuck found himself rooting for the tall, lanky newcomer.

Billy preached for about twenty minutes and then gave a simple invitation for those who wanted to commit their lives to Christ to come forward. Hundreds of young people responded. Templeton was impressed.

For the remainder of 1945, Billy crisscrossed the United States to speak at Youth for Christ rallies. Often Templeton accompanied him, and the two good-looking young speakers found a welcome reception wherever they preached. Hundreds of people responded to their messages of hope and salvation nearly every night.

Templeton remained the star, but Billy proved a strong closer, picking up every night on the themes of despair and hope: "Since this war has ended, people all over the world have been searching for answers. The innocence of our time has passed. The simple life that America has known is gone forever. The simple answers have now given way to much more complex questions. However, let it be known tonight that the ultimate answer has not changed. The answer to man's dilemma is found in Jesus. It is found in the important words of Scripture: 'For God so loved the world that He gave His only begotten Son, that whosoever believeth in Him, should not perish, but have everlasting life.' This is not only your great hope, but it is your only hope of salvation. It is your answer to life. All over this auditorium, the Holy Spirit is dealing with your heart. You come! Give your life to Christ."

Backstage each night, Chuck Templeton watched with interest, admiration, and a bit of wistfulness. He wished . . . he really wanted to . . . he longed to believe as simply and as straightforwardly as Billy did. As Chuck stepped into his dressing room while Billy closed the rally with another successful invitation for men and women alike to entrust their lives to Christ, he listened to the remainder of the service on the old mounted speaker in the corner of the room, the dusty muslin material reverberating with the music and the singing of "Just as I Am." Templeton knew what he was hearing. It was not merely the noise of hundreds of people responding to Billy's words. No, it was much more than that. Charles Templeton knew only too well how a handsome face and a strong voice could create a stir in the preaching world. He had done so himself. With a voice that commanded both respect and love, Templeton never uttered an untoward word or a compromising statement, but when he spoke to an audience, he possessed a subtle sensuality that caused women to swoon at his words and men to consider them all the more seriously—and then to respond. He heard something similar through the old loudspeaker as Billy encouraged the audience, "You come. Come now. Your friends will wait. Come."

And Templeton knew that what he was hearing was not merely a preacher but the birth of a career. He buried his face in his hands and sobbed as he heard Billy say it one more time: "Come!"

"I wish I could," Templeton said.

Chapter Thirteen

Deborah Matthews sat spellbound, listening to Charles Templeton tell of his early experiences with Billy Graham. A bit of an agnostic herself, though originally of Jewish descent, she remembered how one of the men she had loved convinced her to convert to Catholicism before marriage. Now she espoused neither community of faith. She believed in God as a nebulous sort of "first cause," but she could not fathom a God with whom she could have a personal relationship. Perhaps that was why she was so fascinated with Templeton's conversion and subsequent walking away from the Christian faith. How could anyone who had experienced such a mystical—she wanted to use the word *supernatural*, but she feared being fired for sure if she did—conversion simply decide one day that it was all bunk, a sham, and not intellectually credible? She had studied Templeton's early life, read several of his books, and as skeptical as she was known to be, she was convinced that Chuck

Templeton had truly been "born again," as the evangelicals referred to it. How could he disavow that? Wasn't that like annulling a marriage? Nice joke; everyone knows you were married, and now with the stroke of a pen, you can pretend that you were never married at all? The cynical reporter in Deborah could not accept that. She had to find the answer. What happened to Charles Templeton that sent him into a spiritual tailspin?

Templeton himself was at a loss when it came to explaining his early acceptance of Christianity, much less his departure from it. Throughout his lifetime, he'd tried to rationalize it in various ways, never satisfactorily for himself or for anyone else. In his later years, he had tried to stress the intellectual questions with which he grappled, purporting that he had not been able to reconcile his questions about God, the Bible, and faith with good, intellectually credible answers. Yet, for years, Templeton had encouraged people to take a leap of faith.

Deborah Matthews felt that she had to understand Templeton's leap away from faith if she were to successfully cast the same sort of doubt on the faith of Billy Graham. She decided to plunge in where few reporters dared to go. "Mr. Templeton, you described earlier for me your dramatic conversion, and you've mentioned that your life was much more interesting than Graham's. Were you a hypocrite? A charlatan? Or did you honestly believe what you were preaching . . . just as Billy did?"

Templeton glared at Deborah, and for a moment she feared that she had crossed a line, that he was going to tear off the microphone and call an end to their filming. But she underestimated him. He was not afraid of her question at all but rather welcomed it.

"My conversion? Ha! A number of facile explanations present themselves: that I yearned for a satisfactory father figure; that I very much wanted to repay my mother for her thirty-two years of loneliness and struggle by accepting her newfound faith; that my adolescent experiences with sex—innocent enough in retrospect— had burdened me with guilt. Who knows? I was nineteen. And for whatever reasons, I went through what is described today as a 'born again' experience.[1]

"I became an evangelist, and in my travels I met Constance Orosco—Connie—a dark-haired, beautiful woman from California. She was of Mexican descent and was a licensed song evangelist in the Church of the Nazarene, my mother's denomination, and mine for some time as well. Three years earlier, she had been contracted by Hollywood's Metro-Goldwyn-Mayer studios as a budding film star, but having been raised in a deeply religious family, she sought a release from the contract and decided to sing in evangelistic campaigns. We met in Grand Rapids, Michigan, where she was the singer and I was the evangelist. I proposed twelve days after we met; we married six weeks later.

"Connie was a woman of extraordinary faith, and together we started from nothing—I had six hundred dollars left from my career as a syndicated cartoonist—and we built a great church in Toronto, Avenue Road Church. We rented a vacated church building for six months at a hundred dollars per month. The night before we opened, I said to Connie and my mother, 'We have a church but no money. We have pews but no parishioners. We have an organ but no music. But I have a feeling this church will come to life!' And it did. Before long, we attracted a thriving congregation, mostly through my preaching, of course.

"Connie was happy because she very much wanted to live in

---

1. Templeton, *An Anecdotal Memoir*, 32.

one place longer than the customary fifteen days of an evangelistic campaign. And I've always enjoyed a challenge, so the sheer excitement, not to mention the work of starting the church from nothing and then seeing it grow—it once caught fire and burned to the ground, and we rebuilt it, bigger and better—all served to assuage some of the doubts that I was already having about my faith."

"You were having doubts long before you ever met Billy Graham?" Deborah asked.

"Oh my, yes. My doubts had nothing to do with Billy. I began to lose my faith in a hamlet in Michigan, where I was conducting a series of services. It was little more than a cluster of houses and stores at a crossroads, yet it had three competing churches. I preached each evening, but there was little to do during the day. It was impossible to establish a relationship with the pastor I was staying with. He was a neurotically shy, shrivel-souled, skinny little man, a secret smoker who reeked of tobacco and whose fingers had a mahogany hue. When anyone spoke to him, his face would flush and the acne he was cursed with would flame. But he had an extensive and eclectic library. It lined the walls of what he called his study, but was actually the dining room.

I spent most of my days in it, reading voraciously. I had read widely since childhood, but seldom any textbooks and always to my own taste. When a biography of Kemal Ataturk, Turkey's astounding dictator—the only man to my knowledge who, having total power, voluntarily surrendered it—engrossed me, I went on a binge with the library's biographies. For a time, George Bernard Shaw fascinated me—especially the prefaces to his plays—and I read them all, skimming the plays themselves. Then it was everything I could find by or about Gandhi, who remains a major influence in my life."

Templeton sighed and seemed to be analyzing his own past choices before continuing his story. "In this dreary Michigan town, I picked up Thomas Paine's *The Age of Reason*. In a few hours, nearly everything I knew or believed about the Christian religion was challenged and in large part demolished. My unsophisticated mind had no defenses against the thrust of his logic or his devastating arguments."

"But you had an experience . . ." Deborah had difficulty saying the words, and had she not mustered her professionalism as a reporter, they would have stuck in her throat. "You had an experience . . . with *God*!" she said more emphatically than she had intended. "Didn't that trump Paine's arguments?"

"One would think so," Templeton admitted. "And had I ceased my reading with Paine, done some research, and attempted to articulate better answers, I may have been able to survive his onslaught of logic."

"So your doubts were exacerbated by your reading? Can Christianity not stand up to such questions? After all, simply because someone doesn't know the answers does not necessarily mean that valid answers don't exist."

Templeton nodded. "True. But remember, I had nothing with which to refute the challenges I found. In the next ten days, I read Voltaire's *The Bible Explained at Last*; Bertrand Russell's *Why I Am Not a Christian*; the speeches of great American atheist Robert Ingersoll, including his "The Mistakes of Moses"; and dipped into David Hume and Thomas Huxley. I read through the days and into the early morning hours. Each night I stumbled lamely through my sermon, drenched in perspiration, desolate of spirit.

"By the end of the two weeks, my course seemed obvious: my

faith was disintegrating, I couldn't remain in the ministry, couldn't possibly continue to preach. I couldn't even pray. I cancelled the few meetings I had scheduled and returned to Toronto, utterly at a loss. There, I wandered in the wilderness of my mind for six weeks, fending off the questions of family and friends, trying to get some bearings. To earn some money, I sold four political cartoons to the editorial page of the Toronto *Telegram*. I was like a boxer who has been stunned and is out on his feet.

"Then, slowly, I began to emerge from the gray befuddlement. Only half believing, I tried again to pray. In hope, I turned again to the New Testament. The way back was tortuous and slow."[2]

"You couldn't pray?" Deborah asked. "But you prayed for people, and God answered your prayers . . . er, I mean, it seemed that your prayers were answered. There were those two people who were healed . . ."

"Oh yes, that." Templeton waved his hand dismissively. "That was several years later, after Connie and I had married and the church had been well established. I never believed in any of that faith healing. But it is the custom of evangelicals to pray for the sick. Jesus' three years of ministry were filled with healings, and when he commissioned the apostles, he commanded them to heal. In the New Testament book of James, there is this injunction: 'Is any sick among you? Let him call for the elders of the church, and let them pray over him, anointing him with oil in the name of the Lord, and the prayer of faith shall save the sick, and the Lord shall raise him up.' That's the general gist of it anyhow."

"And you and Billy Graham believed that?" Matthews probed.

"I don't know about Billy, but I avoided such matters. I had,

---

2. Adapted from Templeton, *An Anecdotal Memoir*, 41–42.

when requested, prayed for the sick many times, never effectually. I never preached on faith healing, seldom referred to it, and was publicly critical of evangelists who majored in it. I regarded it as peripheral and, in the hands of charlatans, dangerous."

"And yet a woman was healed through your ministry?"

"Well, one Sunday afternoon, I went to one of those small, boxlike frame houses common in Toronto's east end, at the request of a woman who attended the church. Her infant daughter had been born deformed. The large muscle on the right side of the neck was attached to the left collarbone, binding the baby's head to the left. As I understood it, there was some conjunction of the muscle and the jugular vein that made it impossible to correct the problem surgically. Once a week, the woman took the infant to the Hospital for Sick Children for muscular rehabilitation. The baby's head was repeatedly twisted to the right to stretch the muscle so that, in later years, she would be able more or less to face the front. The mother was required to repeat the therapy for ten minutes each day, despite the baby's screams.

"Finding it unendurable, she importuned me to come and pray that the infant be healed. I went reluctantly, feeling like a mountebank, a pretender. The baby was in the bedroom in her crib. I put some olive oil on my fingers, knelt with the mother, put my hands on the infant, and prayed. I had no expectation that the child would be healed. With the glib words on my tongue, I was thinking about the woman—about her pain, and about how disheartened she would be when the baby was unchanged and months of agonizing therapy lay ahead.

"At the close, we rose to our feet and returned to the living room. I was questing in my mind for sentiments with which to buoy up her courage and ease her disappointment. We sat for a few minutes, talking, I in a chair and she and her baby on the chesterfield opposite. Suddenly I asked, 'Wasn't the baby's head bound to the left?'

"The baby was looking to the right and then turned to face me.

"The woman fainted, and as she began to slide to the floor, I caught the baby and placed her on the chesterfield. When the woman revived, she was near hysterics. I told her to report what had happened to the hospital.

"Four years later, *New World*, a Canadian version of *Life* magazine, came to me, looking for a story idea. They planned to do a feature in their Easter edition under the heading, 'What My Faith Means to Me.' I sent them to the woman and to the Sick Children's Hospital. They ran the story and a full-page picture of the mother and child, now a young girl and manifestly normal."

Deborah Matthews shook her head. "Amazing," she said. "But that was not the only healing you experienced, was it?"

"Not long afterward, I encountered another instance of instantaneous healing. My aunt, Ada Poyntz, a graduate nurse and my mother's youngest sister, was terminally ill with what was described to me as stomach cancer. Exploratory surgery had revealed that the malignancy was inoperable. She suffered greatly from adhesions and was bedridden. There was little point in her remaining in the hospital, and in those days, before socialized medicine, the costs would have been prohibitive. She was sent home to live out the rest of her days with my mother.

"Mother insisted that I come to the house and pray for Ada. I went, again with reluctance and that sense of embarrassment I invariably felt when asked to pray for healing. I had investigated many claims of faith healing over the years and had never seen any instance that seemed to me authentic. I couldn't account for what

had happened to the baby's neck, but I was by no means convinced that it was a result of divine intervention.

"I placed my hands on my aunt's body and began to pray. The
moment was intensely emotional. My mother was praying and
weeping. My aunt was gasping in an agony of hope, 'Oh, God!
Please! Please, God!' As I was praying, I felt something akin to an
electrical charge flow through my arms and out of my fingers. I
remembered the incident in which the woman suffering from an
issue of blood touched the hem of Jesus' garment and was healed.
Jesus stopped and said, 'Who touched me?' Peter remonstrated
with him: 'What do you mean, who touched you? There's a crowd
pressing us, jostling us.' 'No,' Jesus said, 'somebody touched me; I
felt power go out of me!' I wondered if what I was feeling was what
Jesus had spoken of.

"Afterward, there was the usual mutual encouragement, the
'trying to have faith.' When I returned home, the telephone was
ringing. It was my aunt, who had not been out of bed for weeks.

"'Chuck,' she said, half laughing, half in tears, but far from
hysteria, 'I've been healed. I really have.'

"Mother came on the phone. 'It's absolutely incredible. She's
been walking around. She's been up and down the stairs. Chuck,
she's healed. There's no doubt about it.'

"There was no return of the malignancy. The adhesions
ended. She outlived the rest of her brothers and died forty-two
years later at the age of eighty-seven."

Deborah Matthews shook her head dramatically. "Two cases,
with which you were quite familiar with the details and could follow up; and in both cases, the individuals were healed after you
prayed for them. How do you account for that?"

Templeton laughed. "How do I account for those two instances of apparently instantaneous healing?"

"Yes, how do you?" asked the reporter, noting Templeton's description of the miracles.

"I cannot," Templeton replied. He chuckled gingerly. "They certainly didn't happen because of my faith. Nor do I believe they resulted from divine intervention."

"Then to what do you attribute them?" Matthews asked, with a touch of journalistic sarcasm. "You saw these individuals with your own eyes. You knew these people as being trustworthy."

Templeton shook his head. "Having investigated faith healing over many years, I have no doubt that, occasionally, men and women are healed of actual illnesses. I am not speaking of those illnesses that are hysteric in nature, symptoms of an underlying psychological problem. Nor of those 'healings' that are undoubtedly remission, the temporary subsidence of symptoms or pain. Nor again am I referring to the so-called healings seen on television when the ailing victim is anaesthetized by the intensity of the moment and becomes able, if only for a brief period, to bend a painful back or walk on a crippled limb.

"I am opposed to the public healing services of contemporary evangelism. Occasionally, a form of cure may be effected, but the good is minuscule compared to the harm. Television healing evangelism is a fraud. The 'healers' are often simpletons or rogues or both, living off the avails of medical bunkum. They knowingly mislead, leaving behind them emotional wreckage and illnesses often worsened by neglect.

"Despite all this, I am convinced that what may loosely be called faith healing is an area of medicine with unrealized potential."[3]

---

3. Adapted from Templeton, *An Anecdotal Memoir*, 44–47.

"That's a very curious analysis, Mr. Templeton," Matthews said. "I'd love to explore that further with you sometime, but let's get back to Billy. You said that you liked him immediately when you first met."

"Of course," Templeton replied. "We became friends, but we were more than that. We were like brothers. We traveled together . . . preached together. It was impossible not to . . . *like* Billy."

"And he genuinely liked you . . ." Deborah led Templeton.

"Absolutely. I've read that Billy Graham said I am the only man he ever loved."

"Oh, really?" Matthews replied. "Now, that's interesting."

Templeton scowled at the reporter. "Yes, we went everywhere together. You know we even went to Europe right after the war . . . let's see . . . I believe that was late 1945 or 1946; you can check it. Billy and I went along with four other evangelists, and Torrey Johnston, if you can call him an evangelist. Torrey organized the forty-six-day trip as part of an effort to expand Youth for Christ to Europe. The plan was for Billy and me to alternate doing the preaching; a robust baritone named Stratton Shufelt would supply the special music. For most of us, it was our first trip abroad. It wasn't exactly a luxury flight. We flew over in a DC-4 or a DC-6, a military-type plane, and that plane wrenched more than our backs. I, for one, could barely hold down any food until we arrived in London.

"Great Britain had been decimated by the war, and London in particular had been hit hard by continuous German bombings. Blasted-out buildings were everywhere, and food was in short supply. Rationing was still in place.

"To our surprise, when we got to our hotel, we discovered that we were booked at one of the most expensive hotels in the city.

Billy and I were led to a suite that seemed to us as big as a football field. We looked at each other, eyebrows raised, and began a tour of the rooms.

"Billy called out from the bathroom, 'Chuck, come here!' He was examining the bidet, turning the faucets, looping the spray. 'What is this thing?' he asked.

"I didn't confess my ignorance, but offered what seemed a logical guess: 'It's a footbath.' Just then the telephone rang. It was Torrey. 'What's the extra thing in the bathroom?'

"Billy replied with lofty superiority, 'It's for washing your feet. What'd you think?'

"We held meetings in London, Glasgow, Dublin, and Belfast, as well as numerous other places in Europe. Billy and I roomed together on that entire trip, and we became close friends. We went everywhere together and had a lot of fun. Among a people spent by the long war, we were a curiosity and, I may say, a tonic. In loud-patterned sports jackets, slacks, and bow ties, Billy, Torrey, and I—six feet tall or better and imbued with overabundant energy—intrigued both the clergy and the people. In retrospect, I'm embarrassed at the thought of how brash we must have appeared, but our hosts welcomed it."

"All that sounds so Pollyanna now, sir," Deborah Matthews suggested, "but I've read that seeing the devastation of the war destroyed what little faith you had left. Tell us about that."

A pained expression crossed Templeton's face. "In the months following our return from Europe, I had been fighting a losing battle with my faith. I had been so frenetically busy that there had been little time to take stock. But in the occasional quiet moments, questions and doubts resurfaced. There was a shallowness to what we were doing in Youth for Christ, a tendency to equate success with numbers. There seemed to be little concern with what happened to the youngsters who responded to our appeals. If the after-service dragged on, we tended to get impatient, wanting to wrap things up and get back to the hotel, or to a restaurant for our nightly steak and shop talk.

"Billy, too, was troubled by it, and we talked about it many times. It undoubtedly contributed to his move from Youth for Christ to conduct his own campaigns.

"But my dilemma was of a different kind. I was discovering that I could no longer accept many of the fundamental tenets of the Christian faith. I had been converted as an incredibly green youth of nineteen. I had only a grade-nine education and hadn't the intellectual equipment to challenge the concepts advanced by my friends and mentors. I wanted very much to believe: there was in me then, as there remains now, an intense, innate longing for a relationship with God. In the beginning I accepted the beliefs of the people around me, but I read widely in every spare minute: on planes and trains and in bed. Slowly—against my will, for I could perceive the jeopardy—my mind had begun to challenge and rebut the things I believed . . .[4]

"The war . . ." Templeton brushed a tear from his eyes. "Yes, the war took a toll . . ."

ဆာ

ON TOUR, 1945

Billy and Chuck sat in a movie theater, hoping to relax for a few hours while on the evangelistic circuit. Since both young men

---

4. Templeton, *An Anecdotal Memoir*, 67.

were connoisseurs of movies, today, as they often did when they
got a chance for a break from Torrey Johnson's rigorous schedule,
they had made a beeline to the local theater. As always during the
war years, prior to the feature attraction, the Movietone newsreel
brought American theatergoers film news of what American soldiers were experiencing at the front.

Billy and Chuck had entered the theater lightheartedly, cracking jokes and anticipating a good time. But the film on the screen
quickly arrested their attention as the Movietone newsreel presented graphic film of American soldiers liberating Jewish prisoners
from Auschwitz. The grotesque, stomach-wrenching scenes were
almost unbearable to watch.

"Dear Lord!" Billy gasped as the cameras panned across stacks
of human bodies and opened common graves.

"This can't be . . ." Chuck remonstrated.

Billy gulped hard and looked at Chuck in the dimly lit theater. He felt relieved to divert his eyes from the scenes on the
screen for a moment. "At least the war is over and these people are
saved," Billy offered.

Chuck was virulent. "Saved? At least the war is over? Is that all
you can say?"

"Charles, whattaya mean? The war is over. No more death; no
more destruction."

A middle-aged man in front of Chuck and Billy turned
around and growled, "You wanna keep it down?"

Billy turned and nodded at the man as Chuck continued. "It
isn't that simple, Billy. Are you looking at what I'm looking at?"

The insolent man in front of them answered for Billy. "I said,
'Keep it down!'"

Impulsively, Chuck got up and stormed out of the theater.

"Charles?" Billy called, following after him.

At the back of the theater, Chuck pushed the swinging door open, and he and Billy stepped outside.

"Chuck, what's the matter?" Billy asked.

"What's the matter? I'll tell you what's the matter. Can you look me in the eye and tell me there's a loving God after seeing that?"

"Yes, of course there's a loving God. That's why the war is over. That's why those people have been liberated, saved."

Chuck was irate. "Billy, you saw hundreds being saved. I saw bones, bodies, thousands of people dead!" He paused to let his words sink in. "What loving God would allow that?"

Billy looked back at Chuck, shocked, almost dazed, by the sudden change in his friend's demeanor. "Chuck . . . I don't even want to think that—"

Chuck interrupted him. "Think about it, Billy. Dare to think about it."

Chapter Fourteen

THE GRAHAM HOME, JANUARY 1945

Weary, Billy and Chuck trudged into the Graham apartment, lugging their heavy suitcases. They'd been gone for several weeks, speaking at various venues across the country in Youth for Christ rallies. Both of them were physically exhausted yet exhilarated at the responses of the crowds to whom they had spoken. Youth for Christ was taking off nationwide, and already Billy and Chuck were booked for more events than either of them had imagined.

"I'm home!" Billy called. "Ruth? Chuck is here with me. I've invited him for dinner."

"I'm in your office," Ruth responded.

Billy and Chuck dropped their suitcases near the laundry basket and continued through the hall to Billy's office, one of the rooms at the back of the apartment. Ruth Graham was standing on a stepladder, stretching a tape measure across the windowsill, measuring for curtains as the men entered the room.

"Hi," Billy greeted her. "Oh, be careful there. What are you doing anyhow?"

Ruth carefully climbed down off the stepladder and, with the tape measure still in her hands, threw her arms around Billy. "Welcome home!" She noticed Chuck standing in the doorway. "Oh, hello, Chuck. Come in."

"Hello, Ruth," Templeton said. "I hope I'm not interrupting. Your husband invited me for dinner."

"What were you doing up there on the ladder?" Billy asked again.

"Oh, just measuring for curtains," Ruth answered with a bit of mischief in the sound of her voice.

"Oh, I don't need curtains, honey," Billy said.

"They're not for you," Ruth replied mysteriously.

"Not for me? Well, then who are they for? It's my office."

"Not for long," Ruth teased.

"What do you mean, not for long? I have to have a place to work—"

"They're for the nursery," Ruth said, nodding slightly.

Billy was still thinking about the constant supply of sermons he must write, the study time he needed. "I mean, I gotta have a place to write . . . to prepare sermons and—" He stopped suddenly, as though Ruth's words had finally connected in his mind. "Nursery?"

Ruth nodded her head and smiled.

"Nursery like for plants?" Billy quipped.

"Like for babies," she said with her eyes twinkling.

"Like for *baby* plants?"

Chuck decided to come to Billy's rescue. "*Ahem.* I believe we are discussing human reproduction," he pontificated. "I think she's trying to tell you that you are going to be a father, knucklehead."

Billy looked at Ruth's radiant face. "Do you mean . . . ?"

Ruth nodded again, smiling as Billy swept her off her feet in a gigantic hug and kiss. "Oh, Ruth," Billy said. "I love you. I love you so much." Still holding Ruth off the ground, Billy looked over at Templeton. "Chuck, I'm going to be a father!"

Templeton nodded and smiled broadly. "I guess there is a loving God after all," he said softly to himself as Billy continued to shower Ruth with kisses.

 భ

The months whisked by for Billy and Ruth, partly because of baby preparations, and partly because Billy was traveling for Youth for Christ and preaching everywhere, it seemed—from Moody Church in Chicago to Princeton Theological Seminary in New Jersey. Ruth didn't want to stay alone in Chicago, with Billy being away so much, so the couple moved in with Ruth's parents in the close-knit community of Montreat, North Carolina. Since it was impossible to go back to China in the aftermath of the war, Ruth's father had returned to practicing medicine in nearby Asheville, so besides having her parents for company, she also benefited from excellent medical care.

Ruth joined Billy in various places during the pregnancy, and they always enjoyed window shopping for "baby items." Billy tried to work his speaking schedule around the baby's arrival, but on September 21, with Billy scheduled in Mobile, Alabama, Ruth said, "Billy, I think the labor pains have started." She didn't want him to make the trip.

"Oh, I don't think so," Billy said confidently. "I think it will still be another week or two."

Billy was wrong. Later that evening, Ruth went into labor.

Billy got back from Mobile as soon as he could, arriving at the maternity ward along with T. W. and Chuck and promptly engaging in the one activity he thought would help—pacing the corridor. T. W. and Chuck watched while Billy paced anxiously.

"I do believe you've walked more miles in this corridor than we've traveled in the last year," Chuck said. "Why don't you take a break?"

Billy sat down next to Chuck and tried to keep from fidgeting. He lasted about ten seconds before he jumped back up and began pacing again.

Finally, an obstetrician appeared in the waiting room doorway. "Mr. Graham?" Billy followed the doctor into Ruth's room, where the midwife and nurses were still attending to her. T. W. tagged along behind, but Chuck stayed back by the door, remaining partially out in the hallway.

Ruth looked positively radiant, lying in the bed, holding their infant. She looked up at Billy and smiled. "Come and meet your daughter, Daddy!"

Billy could barely speak. As he looked at their little girl, he could only say, "Hello, darlin'; hello, precious," over and over.

"Go on, Billy," T. W. encouraged him. "Hold her."

Billy reached down and picked up Virginia Leftwich Graham—Gigi, as the family would call her, the first of five Graham children, including Anne, Bunny, Franklin, and Nelson Edman (Ned)—and said, "That's the cutest baby I've ever . . ." That was as far as he made it before becoming overwhelmed. "My daughter . . ." he finally managed to say. He turned toward T. W. and Chuck, standing in the doorway. "My daughter!" he said, raising Gigi like a glass for a toast.

"Congratulations, Billy," Chuck said. "Congratulations, Ruth."

Billy looked at Ruth, "Oh my! In all the excitement, I almost forgot to ask. How are you feeling, Ruth?"

Ruth smiled as she took his hand. "How do you think?"

"Oh."

"I'm fine, Billy. But our baby is . . ." She paused mischievously before saying, "Perfectly wonderful!"

"Perfectly wonderful!" Billy gushed.

Just then, Chuck looked down the corridor to see several doctors running to take care of a young woman being wheeled in on a gurney. The woman was covered with blood as two red-spattered nurses were trying desperately to help keep her alive. Speaking so only he could hear, Chuck murmured, "How can there be a God in this evil world?"

Chapter Fifteen

TEMPLETON'S HOSPITAL ROOM, 2001

The cameraman was furious as he watched the gaffer searching through his accessories bag for a new battery. "Didn't you charge the batteries last night?"

"Yeah, I did . . . I don't know why they didn't take a full charge."

Deborah Matthews looked at Charles Templeton and smiled, then turned to glare at the two tech guys. If looks could kill . . .

"Please tell me this is not happening," she moaned, her anger turning to despair.

"It's okay," the cameraman said, slamming a fresh battery into the slot on the camera's battery pack. "We're cool. We're rolling. Let's just endslate this."

Deborah flashed a fake smile at the cameraman and turned back to the man in the bed. "Mr. Templeton? Can you go back to the part where you were telling us about your questions and doubts?"

"Yes, of course," Templeton replied, swishing at several strands of hair that had fallen across his forehead. "I had profound doubts, and I let my doubts guide me to questions that I could not answer. I let Europe and the aftermath of World War II wash over me. That's what I did. But Billy? His faith was unshaken by what he saw. How can that be?

"I've often wondered if it didn't have something to do with Billy meeting up with that Welshman."

"A Welshman?" Deborah Matthews scribbled a note on her yellow pad.

"Yes, what was his name? Oh, Olford, Stephen Olford."

"What about him? What influence did he have on Billy Graham?"

"Billy met him during our initial trip to Europe, but then when Billy returned to Europe the following year, he and Olford really struck up a friendship. I suppose you could say it was more like a mentorship than a friendship, with Olford being the teacher and Billy the student, even though Olford was about the same age as Billy."

"What was Olford teaching him?" Deborah asked.

"He was something of a preacher himself," Templeton replied. "An evangelist, born to missionary parents; he grew up in Zambia and Angola. Later, as an adult, Olford had what he called 'an encounter with the Holy Spirit.' I never really understood what in the world he was talking about." Templeton paused. "Christians believe that the Holy Spirit is the third person of the Trinity, you know."

Deborah smiled. "I remember something like that from my catechism classes. I never understood how three people could be one person."

"You're not alone, young lady," Templeton said with a laugh. "All the analogies break down when you press them to their extremes or attempt to extrapolate some logic from the concept. I've heard them all: The Trinity—Father, Son, Holy Spirit—is like water in its various forms: ice, liquid, and steam. It is all one part hydrogen, two parts oxygen; it simply exists and functions in different forms. Or the Trinity is similar to the different types of roles you play in life, as a father, son, and husband. Bah! That one made no sense to me at all."

"Do you mean to tell me that Billy understood this concept— this idea of a Holy Spirit—and you did not?" Deborah was genuinely surprised that Templeton would admit his ignorance on such an important aspect of the Christian religion.

"I don't know how much Billy understood," Templeton shot back. "All I can tell you is that in a flytrap of a hotel in the Welsh mining town of Pontypridd, Billy had some sort of experience. He had been preaching at a church near Olford's home—certainly not a venue the size and significance of those we visited when I was along on the trip—and not surprisingly, his Youth for Christ–style sermons were not being well received by the locals. Billy preached each night, but spent each day talking with Stephen Olford. They talked about all sorts of aspects of Christianity, from what I understand, and Olford revealed to Billy that the quality and consistency of his Christian life had been significantly changed by an experience he had with the Holy Spirit while praying a few months before Billy's arrival in Wales. Billy didn't know what that meant, or what to think of his friend's experience, but if it was possible to have a stronger faith, Billy wanted it.

"Now, understand, this is just hearsay; I wasn't there, but later on, Billy and others told me that something highly unusual occurred as Billy and Stephen prayed together one afternoon."

Deborah was intrigued. "Oh? Really? What was that?"

"Well, mind you, I wasn't there . . . but from what I understand, Billy expressed a desire to have a similar experience with the Holy Spirit as Olford had enjoyed. So the two of them knelt in prayer, and Billy began to ask God to do something more in him. He said something like, 'I'm handing my life over to You, God,' and then he kept repenting and asking God to fill him with the Holy Spirit— whatever that meant." Templeton looked up at the reporter. "You know, people were filled with the Holy Spirit on the day of Pentecost, fifty days after Jesus had died and was supposedly raised from the dead. One hundred twenty of those early believers shared an amazing experience in which they heard a mighty, rushing wind, and saw something that looked like tiny tongues of fire coming down and resting above each one of their heads. They started praising God and speaking in languages they had never learned! Can you imagine that?"

"Actually, I can't," Matthews replied. "But it does sound fascinating. Are you telling me that Billy Graham spoke in tongues . . . like some of those Christians I see on television nowadays? They act rather strangely if you ask me."

Templeton's eyes flashed. "I'm not saying anything of the sort. Knowing Billy, I'd rather doubt it. But something happened; of that we can be sure. I told you, I wasn't there. I don't know what Billy did or didn't do, or what he experienced."

"I'm sorry, sir. I didn't mean to put words in your mouth. But you implied earlier that this experience had a profound impact on Billy's faith. You said that your faith was shaken after the war, and his was not. You seemed to attribute at least part of that to this incident with Olford. Were there any tangible results of his 'experience' with the Holy Spirit?"

Templeton nodded thoughtfully. "He read the Bible more . . . Billy had always read the Bible. For as long as I had known him, he had made it a practice to read some portion of the Bible every day, but now he was not merely reading for information. It was 'life' to him; it seemed as though he couldn't live without it."

The reporter looked disappointed. "That's interesting, Mr. Templeton. But forgive me if it sounds a bit mundane and nondescript, especially after such a seemingly significant spiritual experience in Mr. Graham's life. You men were, after all, evangelists. One would expect the Bible to be important to you. Did you notice any other outstanding changes in Billy after his meeting with Stephen Olford?"

Templeton's lips formed a half smile as he looked into Deborah's eyes. She really didn't know much about genuine spirituality, he realized, or where the true battle lines were drawn. But she was a delightful woman, and he enjoyed reminiscing with her. He took a deep breath and thought again about what had happened to Billy, the changes in him after his experience with the Holy Spirit, as Olford put it.

"Yes, his preaching . . . his preaching was different when he came home from Europe the second time. It was as though he had found a new power source. In fact, Olford said later that Billy's preaching changed overnight while he was in Wales. One night, nothing; the people were bored stiff. Then he had this 'experience,' or whatever you want to call it, and the following night, when Billy gave the invitation, offering to introduce people to Christ, the entire audience in that little church responded."

"Did you notice anything different?" Matthews probed.

Templeton shrugged and then rubbed his chin. "As a matter of fact, I did. He seemed to be much bolder when he came back from Europe. I attributed that, of course, to gaining more experience overseas; he was gone for quite a while, preaching almost every night. And when he came home and we hit the trail together again, Billy seemed to be stronger in the pulpit, bigger somehow. I can't really explain it. He seemed to be going for a certain magnificence of effect. It was actually quite fascinating, really impressive, to watch him. He didn't preach any new truths, maybe a little louder, perhaps with more restrained gestures than before, but he always made a beeline to the cross. Billy loved to talk about that cross. And then when he gave the invitation, people responded. Fascinating, I tell you. I was always impressed with the way people responded to his preaching—don't misunderstand; I was never impressed with his preaching—but those people walking down the aisles . . . wherever we went . . . every night . . . regardless of the circumstances. The Holy Spirit?" Templeton shrugged again. "I don't know, but he surely had something . . .

"And then when we came back from Europe—well, here's another thing that always puzzled me. There was an elderly gentleman, a Dr. Riley. He was the president of Northwestern Bible College. Now, I'm not saying it was Harvard, but it was working toward being an accredited college, an institution of higher learning. And this old gentleman, Dr. Riley—God only knows why, if you'll forgive the manner of speaking—says to Billy Graham, 'I'm an old man; I'm dying. I want you to take over as president of the college.'" Templeton crossed his arms over his chest. "Billy Graham? President of a college? Humph! He had a bachelor's degree from Wheaton College . . . in anthropology, of all things! That's it. And all of a sudden, there he is—the youngest college president in the

United States. Through merit? Through scholarship? No! I tell you,
I was the true scholar! If anyone was going to . . ." Templeton shook
his head. "Ahh, I just don't understand . . ."

NORTHWESTERN SCHOOLS,
MINNEAPOLIS FALLS, 1948

Billy had never wanted to be an educator—not in the formal
sense, anyhow. He did have a passion for seeing young men and
women learn how to better communicate the gospel to the world,
and perhaps that is why he accepted the position of president of
Northwestern when the school's leader passed away.

Northwestern had originally been founded as a systematic
Bible school in 1902 by Dr. W. B. Riley, pastor of a large Baptist
church in Minneapolis and a persuasive figure both as a preacher
and an educator. Riley was an intellectual preacher who had
earned a degree from Southern Baptist Seminary at a time when
many ministers had barely more than a Bible Institute education.
He saw the importance of integrating mind and spirit as well as
any Christian educator in America. Not surprisingly, he helped
Northwestern to become a liberal arts college and was pushing the
school toward formal accreditation at the time of his death.

Dr. Riley had first met Billy at Florida Bible Institute, where
he and his family escaped the grueling Minnesota winters for a few
days each year and where he often spoke as a guest lecturer. When
he heard Billy preach at a Youth for Christ rally in Minneapolis
Auditorium in February 1945, Dr. Riley was thrilled to see more
than forty young people respond to Billy's invitation to become
Christians. In his mid-eighties, Dr. Riley became convinced that

Billy was to be his successor, despite his lack of postgraduate degrees. He contacted Billy, invited him to his home, and at eighty-six years of age and barely able to raise his head off his pillow, insisted that Billy succeed him. "You are the man," Riley said, lifting his arm and pointing at Billy.

"Dr. Riley, I can't accept this responsibility," Billy told him respectfully. "God hasn't shown it to me. But if it will ease you, I'll take it on an interim basis until the board can find a permanent president." In October 1947, Dr. Riley informed Northwestern's board that his choice to succeed him was Billy Graham. A guest at Dr. Riley's request, Billy explained his position to the board. "I have no clear indication from the Lord that I am to succeed Dr. Riley," said Billy. "God has called me into evangelism. I have a definite responsibility and commitment to Youth for Christ for the present. However, if it would be any help, I would be glad to become interim president in case of an emergency until the board could make some disposition of the office." For his part, Dr. Riley remained convinced that with a good staff around Billy, and some solid professors, the college would flourish.

Sure enough, when Dr. Riley died in December 1947, the board followed through with the founder's wishes, and Billy Graham became the youngest college president in America, having graduated only four years earlier himself. With Ruth pregnant with their second child, Billy decided to continue living in North Carolina and commute to Minneapolis. Fortunately, Dr. Riley left two highly qualified women who kept the school going in Billy's absence— Marie Riley, the founder's widow, whose presence on campus gave a sense of continuity and stability; and Dr. Riley's longtime secretary, Luverne Gustavson. Luverne knew Dr. Riley's heart and mind as well as anyone, and she helped Billy deal with the myriad details of running a college. Billy also convinced T. W. and his wife to move to Minneapolis to help keep an eye on things at the school. T. W. Wilson, who had no more of an academic background than Billy, became vice president of Northwestern.

Between crisscrossing the country for speaking engagements and the birth of Anne Morrow Graham in May 1948, Billy spent as much time as he could at the college—which wasn't much. He loved the faculty and students though, and tried his best to present himself as a college president. He'd breeze into the busy office, dressed in a stiff new suit and carrying a briefcase, and attempt to deal with fund-raising matters and other problems endemic to a small, private college. But even when he was immersed in work, Billy remained restless. There was a lost world "out there," and it was difficult for him to sit behind a desk when his true passion was evangelism.

−

"Yes, sir," Luverne Gustavson said into the telephone as Billy came through the door of the office. "I'll get that right to you." Luverne had barely hung up the telephone when it started ringing again. She waved at Billy as he approached her desk before entering his office. "Office of the president. Can you hold, please?" Luverne pressed the hold button and grabbed a stack of pink message slips. "Welcome back, sir," she said to Billy. "There've been a lot of calls, Mr. Graham." She handed the wad of messages to Billy and depressed the hold button again. "Yes, this is President Graham's office. How may I assist you?"

Billy smiled as he walked past Luverne's desk and into his office. He should be answering the phone for her, he thought.

President Gustavson's office. Luverne was the one who really ran things around Northwestern.

T. W.—Vice President Wilson—was waiting for Billy in the office. He had been working on the arrangements for Billy's upcoming speaking engagements.

"Hi, T. W. Is everything set for Augusta?"

"It's a go," T. W. responded. "And we've got interest from Modesto, California, and Altoona, Pennsylvania, as well."

"What about Charles?" Billy asked. "Is he on board with this?"

"I'm, um . . . not sure. But look at this." T. W. held up the latest issue of *American* magazine. On the front cover was a full-page, spectacular photo of Charles Templeton onstage at the Los Angeles Shrine Temple. Billy looked at it with interest. "Listen to this," T. W. said as he pointed to the headline on the magazine. "'Religion's Super Salesman.'" T. W. looked up at Billy. "Can you believe it? Where's your picture?"

Billy smiled at his friend's defensiveness. "That's not the point, T. W. It's not about me," Billy said, shuffling some papers on his desk. "And there's no doubt about it, Charles is the greatest evangelist of our age."

Luverne poked her head inside the doorway. "Excuse me, Mr. Wilson. I think you should field this one." She passed a pink slip of paper to T. W. The vice president read it and nodded, so while T. W. picked up the telephone, Billy reached for the magazine with his best friend's picture on the cover. He idly thumbed through the pages till he found the article. It did look interesting.

T. W. put his hand over the receiver and whispered excitedly to Billy. "It's Los Angeles. They want you for those three weeks in September. It's their third call. They need an answer."

"I don't know about L.A." Billy put his hands together tent-style, as though praying. "If Charles isn't on board, nobody knows me out there. A campaign with no people showing up . . . I'd be a laughingstock. It could ruin us."

T. W. nodded and went back to the phone call. "Yes, sir," he said into the mouthpiece. "We're mighty interested. Of course we are. But I'll have to call you back with a confirmation. What? Yes, today. By the close of business today. Thank you."

T. W. hung up the phone and looked at Billy. "We've got two hundred businessmen ready to organize. The support is there."

Billy wasn't so sure. "But we've only got seven thousand dollars for a total budget. Los Angeles needs a budget of twenty-five thousand dollars. I don't see how we can promote a campaign there for anything less."

T. W. raised his eyebrows. "No room for compromise?"

"We can't, T. W. We need Charles. Or we need more money to do it right."

℘

TEMPLETON'S HOSPITAL ROOM, 2001

Deborah Matthews was visibly excited as Templeton reached for a glass of water. "So it really was all about the money to Graham?" she said.

Templeton flared. "Have you not heard a word I've said, young woman? It was *never* about the money for Billy Graham. Or for me either, for that matter. Neither of us cared a whit about money. We lived comfortably; our families were well cared for . . . that's all that we needed. Billy didn't even take a salary from that college in Minneapolis. And early on, in my own ministry, I put myself on salary to avoid the appearance of avarice. Billy did the same."

"But wasn't there some sort of a scandal? A photo of Billy Graham with a sack full of money on the cover of the *National* magazine?"

"Oh, that." Templeton waved his hand and sighed. "That was nothing. In those days the final offering of an evangelistic campaign—they used to call it the 'love offering'—would go to cover the evangelists' expenses and help finance the next campaign. In my ministry, the final collection of the campaign often exceeded five thousand dollars, which would make my annual take around a hundred thousand. That was big money for those days. Too big.

"So some reporter takes a picture of Billy along with some happy campaign workers holding up big bags filled with the love offering from the Atlanta meetings. It made the local newspapers and then the magazine. It was nonsense. But it emphasized to Billy the need to be on a fixed salary. As I recall, his first salary was fifteen thousand a year—mine was half that. I told Billy to make sure that he was accountable for every penny. Completely transparent. And he was. He could have been a multimillionaire simply from the sale of his books. And no one would blame him. He earned the money.

"But when Billy and his group were in Modesto, California, he told his whole team—"

"Sorry," the cameraman interrupted. "I need to change tapes."

Deborah's eyes shot darts at the cameraman, but she maintained her composure. "Okay, hold that thought, Mr. Templeton, please."

The cameraman quickly slapped a new tape into the camera.

"Sorry," he apologized again. "Won't happen again. We should be good the rest of the way out."

Deborah nodded and turned back to Charles Templeton. "You were saying that in Modesto . . ."

"Yes, at their hotel in Modesto, Billy took his whole team and said, 'Now, look, boys; I want you to go to your rooms and each of you write down the things that can cause the downfall of an evangelist.' So they went to their rooms, and they wrote, and then they reconvened. And they all had basically the same items: sex, money, envy, and dishonesty.

"So Billy said, 'All right, from this moment on, here are the rules: none of us is ever going to be alone in a room with a woman other than our wives. We're not going to let there be even a breath of scandal in this ministry. We're going to be strict on salaries and not take a penny more. We're never going to inflate the numbers of people who come to our meetings, and we're never going to gossip about other ministries.'

"Frankly, I've been impressed, though not surprised, by the integrity of Billy and the closest people around him. Especially when you think of some of the scandals that have plagued Christianity down through history. But not a breath of scandal about Billy Graham. Not a breath.

"Mind you, I disagree vehemently with his preaching. But he is the most scrupulously honest person I've ever met. There's not a thing phony about him. He's the genuine article. And when I needed a friend, he was always there."

Chapter Sixteen

CONNIE AND CHARLES TEMPLETON'S HOME,
SPRING 1949

Connie and Chuck Templeton sat alone in their home, having a serious, contemplative conversation. Connie had known for some time that Chuck was troubled and experiencing grave doubts about his faith. She also knew that like many hurting pastors and evangelists, he had nobody to whom he could safely go for help. No one to talk to, nobody who would understand, not one soul who would hold his doubts in confidence. After all, how does a man who tells thousands of other people how to find faith confess that he is struggling with his own? How can he admit that he is questioning everything he once so wholeheartedly believed, trying to make intellectual sense of his faith and finding himself grasping at fog? To whom does such a man go for help or advice?

Not surprisingly, Chuck's inner spiritual turmoil produced

physical problems as well. In tip-top condition for most of his life, suddenly, in his mid-thirties, Chuck began to experience pains in his chest, shortness of breath, and numbness throughout his forearms and hands. The first consideration, of course, was heart disease. But after extensive testing, Chuck's doctor could find no evidence of a heart problem—not a physical heart problem, at least. "Ease up; slow down; take a vacation," he was told, but the symptoms persisted.

Ironically, about the same time that Chuck was hanging on to his faith by a thread, the media took a tremendous interest in him, extolling his successes in magazine and newspaper articles. NBC-TV invited Chuck to do four thirty-minute television programs from Chicago. Yet even as he grappled with his own misgivings about Christianity, people who had found strength or faith through listening to him looked at him in awe and gratitude. Their adulation only served to make Chuck more self-conscious about the dichotomy between the person he was on the platform and the one he knew himself to be at all other times. As he later described his condition, "It was not that I disbelieved; it was simply that my mind was at war with my spirit."[1]

During a most successful campaign in Harrisburg, Pennsylvania, Chuck's physical problems increased. His nights were bedeviled by fear, intense perspiration, and a strong pounding in his chest. Chuck finally sought out a heart specialist who had attended his services and asked the doctor to examine him. The doctor did a thorough exam and then shocked Chuck with his conclusions. "There's nothing wrong with your heart," he said. "Nothing. The pains are the result of a heart spasm. But the trouble isn't in your

---

1. Templeton, *An Anecdotal Memoir*, p. 85.

heart; it's in your head. There is something in your life that is bothering you. Some conflict. Some unresolved problem. Whatever it
is, deal with it. Otherwise, you will probably continue to suffer the
symptoms you have described and will likely see other manifesta-
tions as well."

Chuck knew what the problem was, but he dared not discuss
it with the doctor—the doctor who had come to hear *him* give
prescriptions for a better life that same week. Connie, of course,
recognized this double-edged sword in her husband's life. There
was only one person, in her estimation, who would not only
understand but to whom Chuck could safely go for help without
fear of risking his reputation and his ministry. "Go see Billy," she
encouraged him.

"How can I go to Billy with my doubts? With my questions?"
Chuck asked.

"Of all the people glad-handing you in Christendom, Billy is
the one who loves you. He is the one you can trust."

Chuck knew that Connie was right. "I don't know where to
begin . . ."

"Just tell him the truth," she urged. "He's a straight shooter.
He knows your heart and will accept your mind with this . . . this
great struggle for answers. Billy wants to reach out to souls like
you. He will understand."

Chuck slowly nodded in agreement. Connie moved closer to
Chuck and touched his hand. They both stood to their feet, their
eyes locked on each other in warmth and tender love. Chuck
touched Connie's face softly, then pulled her to him in an affec-
tionate embrace.

"Thank you, Connie," he whispered as he held on to her
tightly. "For everything, thank you."

~~

BILLY AND RUTH'S HOME, MONTREAT, NORTH CAROLINA,
SUMMER 1948

Chuck Templeton smiled approvingly as he made his way up the narrow mountain road, toward the house constructed of great adze-hewn timbers and secluded on a heavily treed slope at the end of the winding road. "Very nice, Billy," Chuck said aloud. "A haven, a respite from the world . . ." His countenance turned sour. "The perfect place to hide."

Ruth greeted Chuck at the door. "Charles, welcome to our home!"

"Thank you, Ruth," Chuck responded. He stood silently for an awkward moment or two.

"Well, come on in." Ruth took his hand and led him inside the log cabin–looking home. "Billy is in the living room, reading by the fireplace."

"Thank you, Ruth."

Ruth sensed the weight in Chuck's spirit and exited the room as she gestured toward the living room. Chuck followed her lead and stepped toward the living room.

"Chuck! Chuck, good to see you." Billy rose from the chair where he was reading. He slapped his friend on the back as usual, although both men seemed to recognize that this was not an ordinary meeting between the two of them. "Come in; sit down." Billy pointed to a couch near the large fireplace, and the two men sat down together. They exchanged perfunctory pleasantries, asking about each other's families, comparing notes on their latest campaigns. And then silence. The crackle of the fire produced the only sound in the room.

Chuck looked perplexed, as though he was searching for just the right words. Finally, he leaned in toward Billy and spoke earnestly. "Billy, I'm at a crossroads. I have more questions than answers. At times, I feel all alone with my doubts. Sometimes there is more fear and pride than love in my heart."

Billy was utterly perplexed by his friend's statements and made no attempt to conceal his feelings. "What are you talking about, Chuck?"

"Billy, how can anyone take the Bible as the literal Word of God?"

"What? What do you mean?"

The floodgates had burst opened in Chuck Templeton's heart, and his questions and doubts flowed out like an escaping rain-swollen river. "Jonah and the whale? Do you think a whale really swallowed a man and spat him out? Or God making the sun stand still. Do you honestly believe the earth stopped revolving? Where's the hard science to back up these stories?"

Chuck leaned even closer to Billy's face. "And if the Scriptures aren't true in each and every case, doesn't that cast doubt on all of it?"

Billy was astounded and distraught; the pain from Charles's words showed in his face, but he wanted to be helpful to his friend. "Charles," he said, looking Templeton in the eyes, "it's the Word of God."

Templeton flew back at Billy. "But, if part of it is wrong . . . if it is nothing more than feeble stories attempting to answer the great questions of life, then what about the rest?" Templeton shook his head slightly. "Billy, what have we accomplished?

Manipulating crowds with simple stories spun by our skills as orators?"

"Charles!"

Just then Ruth entered the living room, "Tea? Coffee?" she asked merrily.

"No, thank you, Ruth," Charles answered flatly, as though he did not appreciate her intrusion. Billy and Ruth exchanged concerned looks. Ruth decided to exit without a word.

Chuck relaxed a bit, but continued his verbal review of what he had been pondering in his mind for months. "We're a couple of good-looking, dynamic guys. Maybe that's all there is to it. Maybe it is all about just selling what the people want. Brushes. Just like you selling Fuller brushes. Not that they don't need a brush or two to clean up the messes in their lives."

Billy reached out to Chuck and laid his hand on the top of his shoulder. "Charles, every great man of God has been tested. This is a crisis of the spirit. God is allowing you to be put to the test. If you pass this test, you will be given greater responsibility in the kingdom. Don't fail Him now."

A look of sincere pain creased Charles's face. "Oh, Billy, if only I could continue to believe that."

"Believe it," Billy encouraged him. "Charles, look at your career. A career for God! Look at your influence, the crowds you draw. No one ever filled a stadium to sell brushes. The Word of God is doing that. I see that in my ministry. When I try to preach, to tell people what Billy Graham thinks, it falls flat. But when I simply preach the Word of God, it has power, and lives are changed."

For a long few moments, both men remained silent. Finally, Chuck looked into Billy's face and said, "I'm going to Princeton."

"What? You're going back to school?"

"Come with me, Billy," Chuck begged. "I've been successful because of my gifts, because I can move a crowd, not because of my knowledge. Not because of any real scholarship. You and Ruth, come with me."

Billy's mouth was dry. "Charles, I'm the president of a Bible college. I couldn't go to graduate school in the United States. I'd be dishonoring my school and my students."

"Resign then!" Templeton said adamantly. "If you don't, you're committing intellectual suicide, and you know it!"

Billy was silent for a long time. When he spoke, he spoke quietly, thoughtfully. "If we can get accepted to a university outside of the United States, say, Oxford, then I'll go with you. I've had my doubts too, Charles. Everyone does at one time or another. I'm not afraid of knowledge. I welcome it. What do you say we apply to Oxford?" Billy thrust out his hand for his friend to shake on the deal.

Chuck looked at Billy's extended hand as though it were covered with leprosy. "I can't," he said quietly. "I've already been accepted at Princeton."

Billy's face was downtrodden, his countenance sullen. It was done. His friend was leaving him to travel a different path, a road that would likely take them in radically different directions. Billy continued to hold out his hand . . . but Charles Templeton did not take it.

Chapter Seventeen

TEMPLETON'S HOSPITAL ROOM, 2001

Charles Templeton shook his head sadly as he thought back on Billy's outstretched hand, innocently indicating his willingness to attend Oxford or some other school together. Templeton looked up at Deborah Matthews, and the reporter thought for a moment that she saw a tear in the old man's eye.

"I knew I couldn't do that to him," Templeton said softly.

The reporter didn't understand. "Do? Do what? Get more education? What's so awful about that? The man was masquerading as a college president, after all. He *needed* more education. At least you realized that."

"No, dear." Templeton stroked his chin. "Billy didn't need more education to do what he felt called to do. Billy was not concerned about gaining more education. He was concerned about saving souls . . . and saving me . . . saving me from myself. And as his friend, his true friend, I had to save him from me as well."

"I'm sorry, sir. I don't understand."

"I knew Billy well enough that if I had said yes and had taken his hand when he offered it, he would have resigned his position at Northwestern, and probably his position with Youth for Christ as well, and he would have gone to Oxford with me. I have no doubt about that. And if he had, I have no doubt that evangelical Christianity today would be entirely different, and so would Billy Graham." Templeton looked away from the camera, as though looking far in the distant past. When he spoke again, it was in such a soft whisper that Deborah could hardly hear him. "But I *couldn't* take my friend's hand. I could not do that to him. And so he went down one path, and I another . . ."

ɛ⁄ɔ

AVENUE ROAD CHURCH, TORONTO, SUMMER 1949

Chuck and Connie Templeton paused in the narrow stairwell that led up to the platform and pulpit of the Avenue Road Church in Toronto, Canada. The people pouring into the newly rebuilt church thought they were simply attending another service in which they would hear an encouraging and motivating message from their increasingly famous pastor, Charles Templeton. Connie and Chuck knew that such was not to be the case.

As the people crowded into the sanctuary, Connie took her husband's hand. "Charles, I have loved you from the moment your hand first touched my face, and you spoke those words—"

"Shh," Chuck said, turning tenderly toward Connie and touching her lips with his open hand. He gazed into her adoring eyes, then pulled her close to him for a final embrace before he mounted the remaining stairs to the platform. As they pulled apart, the genuine love and mutual respect they shared was obvious, yet it was equally apparent that Chuck's doubts and struggle with his faith had created a strain between them. "I know. In many ways, it was you and your love, Connie, that got me up on that stage, night after night, when I had nothing to give."

"It was more than my love, Chuck. I know you as a man of character, and I fear . . ." She stopped short and her hand drew instinctively to her heart. "I fear now the press will be out to destroy you." Connie brought her husband's hand to her lips and kissed it softly.

"I know, I know," he said quietly. "They're going to call me a traitor, an impostor, a fraud. But more than me, it's you that I worry about. Connie, I cannot bear to have the scorn heaped on you. I know you are a believer . . . a sincere believer."

"Charles Bradley Templeton, I chose to share my life with you. Whether you are making the worst decision of your life tonight or the decision that will set you free, I will be here, by your side." His piercing eyes bore into hers; it was another long look between two souls that had been on a difficult journey together and were about to take a radical turn in their lives. He wished that he could say those same words to her—"I will be here, by your side"—but he knew that his new direction was not one she wished to share.

Connie fought back her tears. "I just have one question."

Chuck looked surprised, taken aback by the penetrating look from a woman who knew her man better than anyone else. For once, the eminently confident, always-ready-with-an-answer Charles Templeton could barely speak. After several seconds, with Connie's eyes gazing into his, he haltingly answered, "Yes, what is it?"

Connie's dark eyes penetrated far deeper into Charles Templeton than he had ever allowed anyone to enter. "Are you sure?" Connie asked quietly. "Are you really sure, Chuck?"

For a brief moment, a look of doubt crossed Templeton's face. Connie refused to release him from her gaze, even though he attempted to pull away. Another long, tense moment and she could tell that his brilliant mind was racing faster than light. For what seemed like hours but was actually only a minute or two, Chuck pondered deeply the consequences of his decision. Then, without a word, he turned and began to walk up the remaining stairs, as the song leader concluded the last song before the sermon. Templeton felt as though his heart and mind were about to explode. He wobbled a bit on the staircase, in such a way that he could have gone in either direction. Then he turned slightly and took a long, final look at his beautiful wife. He pursed his lips, tried to wave good-bye, but could not. Connie nodded, sobbing quietly and fighting back the free flowing of her tears, as the two of them marched up the steps together for the last time. Chuck stepped through the doorway onto the platform as Connie slipped down the front stairs, off the platform, and sat down in the front row. Chuck took a deep breath and approached the pulpit.

Dressed impeccably, as always, in a dapper double-breasted suit, white shirt, and brightly patterned tie, with every strand of his wavy, dark, closely cropped hair in place, he was the picture of ministerial success. He knew that nobody would ever force him to do what he was about to do—nobody could, yet he himself could not do otherwise.

As he looked out at the congregation, he saw the familiar faces of friends, many of whom he had personally led to believe in God and into a relationship with Jesus Christ. He saw couples whom he had pronounced husband and wife. He looked into the eyes of dear, elderly women for whom he had prayed about a wide variety of needs; he saw men who had found purpose and meaning in their lives by trusting in a God of love rather than judgment. He looked at a row filled with teenagers whom he had challenged on numerous occasions to live for something greater, something nobler than the latest fad or the big game. He also saw several adoring women who regularly hung on every word he spoke, enthralled especially when he spoke of love and kindness, and although they had never approached him, he knew several of them who were ready and willing to take Connie's place in his life in a moment—for a lifetime, or simply for the night.

As Chuck Templeton stood silently behind his pulpit, looking out over the congregation he sincerely loved, a reverential hush fell over the room. Chuck opened his mouth, hoping against hope that he could actually utter words intelligibly. He began slowly and somberly. His voice wavered a bit as he said, "I see many familiar faces tonight." He stopped and uncharacteristically cleared his throat before trying again. "I have known some of you since you came into this world." He looked over at the row of teenagers. Several of them returned his gaze, nodded, and smiled.

"I have seen some of you through times that were good, and times that were not so good."

Nervous chuckles and nods from the older people in the audience gave Templeton pause. He attempted a smile, but it appeared more like a grimace. *No matter*, he thought. *I must go on.*

"And together with faith and love, we have built this great church to what it is today." Chuck allowed his eyes to move across the room from one side to the other, looking over the pensive crowd. Several men fidgeted nervously. A few women looked worried as they listened.

Templeton continued slowly and precisely. "It has been my honor and my privilege to serve you." More individuals in the crowd exchanged worried glances.

"But I'm here with heavy heart." Murmurs spread across the congregation. Something was amiss, they knew now.

"You are not just my parishioners. You are my friends. And to all of you, I apologize in advance for the brevity of this talk. Some of you will think I owe you more. And I agree with you. I might owe you more. In me you put your trust for spiritual guidance. I realize the responsibility and honor of this. I realize it to the center of my core."

By now, tears streamed freely down Connie's face. A woman sitting next to her reached over and took her by the hand. Another woman passed a package of tissues to the first woman, who handed them to Connie. Connie thanked her quietly as she removed a tissue and dabbed her eyes. The woman next to her removed several tissues and patted her own eyes.

Chuck took a deep breath and then launched into the essence of what he wanted to say to his loving congregation. "But I find I can no longer accept many of the fundamental tenets of the Christian faith." Chuck Templeton's voice quivered, despite his effort to speak firmly. He knew this was it; like a rowboat on the mighty Niagara River, he had passed the point of no return and was headed for the falls. "I now see that there are other ways, other paths, other perspectives, other truths. And to continue this journey toward greater understanding, toward an ever-widening search for truth, I have decided to go to Princeton University."

Several people in the church gasped. A few recoiled in horror;

some of Chuck's female admirers burst into tears, although they were not alone. Even strong, stoic businessmen felt their mouths go dry and their eyes grow damp as the full ramifications of their pastor's statements began to sink into their minds and hearts.

Chuck stepped back from the pulpit for a moment, desperately trying to collect his thoughts and maintain his composure. He looked in Connie's direction, and their eyes connected. Although she had rightly surmised that the implications of what he was doing would destroy their marriage, she loved him nonetheless, and he loved her.

Chuck took a breath, stepped back to the pulpit, and announced what many of his parishioners had already figured out. "And that means I'm leaving this ministry."

The rowboat plunged over the falls.

Chapter Eighteen

NORTHWESTERN OFFICE, SUMMER 1949

Word of Charles Templeton's resignation swept across the nation. As he predicted, some of his former friends and colleagues quickly labeled him a hypocrite, a huckster, a fraud, and worse. Almost overnight, he became a pariah in some circles, especially among fundamentalist Christians who hastened to say that they had never approved of his message of hope and optimism anyhow, nor did they appreciate his practice of presenting the gospel in more of a challenging, you-should-try-this style of evangelism. Finger-pointing and I-told-you-so's were rampant when Templeton's name was injected in many conversations among conservative Christians. Some called him derogatory names; others called his name in their prayers. Everyone wanted to know how someone like him could disavow the basic tenets of his faith, and the most obvious person to ask was his best friend. His best friend, however, was grappling with his own doubts.

☙

Billy rushed into the Northwestern office with a distracted, pained expression on his face. He passed by T. W. without so much as a greeting. He steered straight for his inner office, oblivious to Luverne Gustavson's presence in the outer office as he passed by. He sat down at his desk and immediately began poring over a pile of books and papers.

"Mr. Graham," Luverne called, clutching a stack of messages.

Billy did not respond.

"Mr. Graham!" Luverne called after him loudly.

Billy snapped his head up; he realized that he had been staring at a row of large, imposing books on his bookcase. He looked up at his secretary as though he were seeing her for the first time that day—which indeed he was. "Oh, I'm sorry, Luverne."

Luverne stood in the doorway between Billy's office and her own. She held an opened letter in her hand, and she scanned the page till she found the information for which she was searching. "You are confirmed at the Forest Home Conference."

"Forest Home?"

"Yes, Mr. Graham. It is the retreat center operated by Henrietta Mears, the director of Christian Education at Hollywood Presbyterian Church, and she has personally extended the invitation. You'll be the youngest college president speaking there. Looks quite interesting. Dr. Evans and Dr. Orr from Oxford will be there."

"Sounds good," Billy said with a nod.

"Oh, and so will your friend, Charles Templeton." Luverne slid the letter across the desk toward Billy, turned on her heel, and went back to her desk.

Billy picked up the letter as though it contained a bomb that might go off at any second. "Thank you, Luverne." He stared at the letter, got up, and closed the office door separating him from his staff. He sat down at his desk and spread the letter out in front of him.

Billy gazed at the letter and then at the bookcase across the room. He rose and reached for several texts: *Totem and Taboo* by Freud; *Varieties of Religious Experience* by William James; *Critique of Pure Reason* by Kant; *Neo Orthodoxy* by Karl Barth; *Being and Nothingness* by Sartre. He carried the books back to his desk, sat down, and began searching the pages.

About that same time, across the country, in the quaint New Jersey town of Princeton, Charles Templeton sat at a large table in the library of Princeton Theological Seminary. Ironically, he had spread before him the exact same books that Billy was perusing.

Late that night, the lights were still on in Billy's Northwestern office. Still at his desk, he sat alone, with his tie loosened, his desk covered with open books, pages of notes strewn in every direction. Stiff from studying so long, Billy leaned back in his chair and stretched as he looked out the window at the night sky. He'd be going back to North Carolina in the morning. He planned to take the books with him and work while he was at home.

The following night, after another cross-country flight, Billy spread out his materials in his Montreat home study. Long after he and Ruth had prayed with the children and kissed them good night, Billy remained at his desk, scouring the theological books he'd brought home from Northwestern, as well as others he had found in his home library.

Trying not to disturb him, Ruth quietly entered the study, bringing Billy a cup of hot tea. She took one look at Billy's desk and let out a slight laugh. "It's as if you are in school again, studying for an exam."

Billy did not crack a smile. "Ruth, I've come a long way. And I don't know if where I am is where I'm meant to be."

"What? What does that mean? What are you talking about, Bill? Me? The kids? This home? What?"

"Oh no; not you. I mean, spiritually."

Ruth looked at him quizzically. "So you're saying you should have remained a dairy farmer?"

"Maybe. I'm questioning everything right now. I'm living in two worlds. I don't know if I'm supposed to be a college president or an evangelist. I feel like a hypocrite. I profess to believe in the full inspiration of the Scriptures, but lately, I'm not sure I can back it up with facts."

Ruth picked up one of the books written by a well-known liberal theologian. She read the flyleaf, then looked at Billy askance. "And this will help?" She tossed the book on the desk dismissively. "Billy . . ."

"Ruth, I cannot simply go out before those trusting audiences unless I have the answers myself."

"I understand," Ruth replied. She moved behind Billy's chair and wrapped her arms around his neck. "The good thing is, God has the answers," Ruth said as she rubbed his shoulders. "Billy, we have lived our lives with the promise that He would never leave nor forsake us. His Word is true. He will speak to you again."

Billy smiled up at her tentatively. "Yeah. I'm just having a little trouble hearing Him lately."

∾

Back at Northwestern the following week, the maelstrom over Charles Templeton's resignation and enrollment at Princeton continued unabated. When Billy returned to the office, Luverne was waiting for him, loaded with a fresh batch of messages. Reporters badgered Luverne constantly, hoping to get an interview with Billy regarding the questions swirling around Templeton. She tried to ignore most of the requests, but Luverne soon ran out of stall tactics, so Billy reluctantly complied with as many interviews as possible.

"Mr. Graham, another reporter is on the line," Luverne announced, interrupting Billy's thoughts. "Shall I take a message?"

In his office, Billy sighed wearily. "This'll be the last one. Put him through."

For the next half hour, a reporter peppered Billy with questions for which he had no answers. All he could say definitively was that Charles Templeton and he were still friends. No, he had not talked to him since the news had broken. Yes, he still believed Charles was a good man. No, he did not plan to make a similar move any time soon.

Dealing with the turmoil in the press was one thing, but coping with the disappointment and disillusionment among his colleagues and the students at Northwestern was far more difficult. As the controversy heated up and people began taking sides, Billy felt that he must address the issue before the student body and the local church members who frequented Northwestern chapel services.

With the chapel full of students as well as visitors who'd happened to hear that the Northwestern president was going to speak about the Charles Templeton affair, Billy stood boldly behind the college pulpit. He had no illusions regarding his task. He knew that this was sure to be one of the most difficult speeches he would ever have to give. Because of the tenseness of the situation, Ruth had accompanied Billy on this trip to Northwestern, a rarity for her, but she felt he needed a little extra emotional support while he handled this situation. She sat on the front row as Billy addressed the crowd.

After a few perfunctory remarks, Billy got straight to the point. "By now all of you will have heard that Reverend Charles Templeton has resigned both from Youth for Christ and from his ministry. Pastors in our church and others have begun to denounce Mr. Templeton for betrayal of the faith. Some have even questioned whether Mr. Templeton ever truly experienced conversion to the Lord.

"He has been called a hypocrite and a huckster."

Billy paused to make sure he had the attention of everyone in the chapel before continuing. "Let me tell you, Charles Templeton is my best friend, and there is nothing dishonest in the man. Because of a crisis of his faith, he felt a moral imperative to resign his positions, to no longer preach that which he could no longer fully believe. That is not hypocrisy; that is integrity."

On the front row, Ruth nodded in agreement.

Billy's voice rose in intensity as he drew his remarks to a close. "I will not join with any who denounce my friend. Instead"—he paused and looked around the faces in the chapel—"let us all pray for him."

છ

PRINCETON, NEW JERSEY, 1948

While Billy continued his vigorous schedule of speaking at Youth for Christ rallies and serving as a figurehead for Northwestern,

Charles Templeton found himself at home at Princeton. His arrival had not been unheralded—having been announced in newspapers across America—and had not gone without some resentment, jealousy, and disdain on the part of other Princetonians. His admission to the school was fraught with oddities, not the least of which was the fact that Templeton had never completed high school, much less earned a bachelor's degree from a reputable, accredited college that would be considered a normal stepping-stone to such a prestigious school as Princeton.

The path to Princeton had indeed been tumultuous for Templeton. Grappling with his own spiritual declension led him to think that the questions in his heart and mind might be resolved if he were able to pursue a more formal theological education. While Chuck had been pastor at Avenue Road Church in Toronto, he discussed that possibility with his friend Canon Arthur Chote, of Toronto's Anglican Church. Templeton had initially met Arthur during Chuck's stint with Youth for Christ. Their relationship solidified further when the woman Chote later married was motivated to become a Christian after hearing a sermon by Templeton.

In the spring of 1948, while Arthur was studying for the ministry at Wycliffe College, he stopped by Chuck's study to visit. In the course of their conversation, Arthur startled Templeton by suggesting that if he wanted to continue to be useful in the ministry, he should quit preaching and return to school. Arthur was not denigrating Chuck's preaching; quite the contrary, Chote admired his friend and appreciated his keen intellectual approach to the Scriptures. He sincerely believed that Chuck would benefit greatly by adding academic knowledge to his already brilliant mind and eloquent elocution skills.

Templeton listened to Arthur intently as he quietly touted the virtues of philosophy and the latest ravings in New Testament studies being extolled by the new brand of postwar theologians known as "neoorthodox." Their "new" orthodoxy, in truth, was little more than ancient Gnosticism wrapped in leftover nihilism, but it appealed greatly to a group of theologians who had lost faith in human beings after the likes of Hitler. Confronted by the reality of evil, they conveniently placed the blame on the Bible and religion's failure to truly transform society—in essence choosing to become willing participants in the proverbial tossing the baby out with the bathwater.

The ideas appealed to Templeton, though at the time, he could not imagine how he could go back to school. Where would he begin? In high school? Correspondence school? And even if he were to obtain further education, what assurance was there that he would be more useful to anybody upon his return to the pulpit—*if* he returned to the pulpit?

After Arthur departed, Templeton remained alone in his study for several hours, brooding, pondering his friend's advice. Templeton had already admitted to himself what Arthur Chote had only sensed—that Chuck's faith in God was dwindling rapidly. He knew that he lacked the theological training to answer even his own questions, much less anyone else's. Perhaps Arthur was right; maybe he would benefit personally and be more of a help to others if he could resolve some of his own misgivings and enter more fully into genuine faith. Late that night, Templeton decided that despite the uproar it might cause, the potential gain was worth the inevitable pain—he would resign from his church, leave Youth for Christ, and seek further formal education.

But how? Where? A friend, Jim Mutchmor, the former head

of the Department of Evangelism and Social Service in the United Church of Canada, suggested that Templeton apply to Princeton, despite lacking the undergraduate degrees necessary for admission. Templeton did so and received an immediate response letter from the academic dean—encouraging him to complete his high school education and earn a degree from an accredited college or university; then Princeton would be happy to consider him for possible admission.

Undaunted, Templeton wrote to the dean, asking if he could present his case to the president of the university. A meeting was set and probably would have yielded the same results had not Dr. George Pidgeon, moderator of the United Church of Canada, been the chapel speaker at Princeton that morning. Following the service, Princeton's president, Dr. John Mackay, mentioned to Dr. Pidgeon that he had another Canadian coming to meet with him later that day—a Charles Templeton. Mackay asked the moderator if he knew Templeton.

"Oh yes; I know Templeton," Dr. Pidgeon replied. "Or I should say, rather, that I know of his work as an evangelist. He draws great crowds to his meetings. If he wants to return to school, please do whatever you can to help him."

Mackay met with Templeton and was unimpressed with Chuck's theological knowledge. "Much room for thinking there," he wryly commented at the conclusion of their interview. But Mackay was impressed with Templeton's seriousness about pursuing knowledge. Oddly, Mackay made Templeton an offer he was sure to refuse: On the basis of his years of preaching experience, he would be admitted as a "special student" to Princeton; he would be required to attend all classes in the three-year theological program, take all examinations, and possibly write a dissertation, but he would *not* be granted a degree from the university, since he did not have the prerequisites.

Mackay sat back in his chair. "What do you say to that?" he asked, certain that Templeton would flee his office, never to return.

"I accept," Templeton replied. "How soon can I enroll?"

∞

As fall set in and the leaves changed colors on the giant oak trees in the Princeton grove, Billy Graham continued to crisscross the country in evangelistic meetings, tossing and turning in hotel beds, struggling with the questions Chuck had posed to him. Meanwhile, Charles Templeton began his theological studies. Templeton acclimated quickly to Princeton, realizing the most important principle of any education: the world of learning is not in the classroom; it is in the library.

Templeton relished the academic environment, especially the interaction with the Princeton faculty members—many of whom were not much older than he was—and the encouragement by his professors to question all assumed truths he had accepted previously. The attitude on campus fostered a spirit of intellectual sparring. Albert Einstein taught at Princeton's Institute for Advanced Study during the time Templeton attended classes at the seminary, and Templeton greeted the quirky genius frequently as he shuffled along the wide campus sidewalks, dressed in frumpy, disheveled clothing. Robert Oppenheimer, the "father of the atomic bomb," also frequented campus, as did other brilliant scholars, speakers, politicians, authors, and doctors. Templeton had finally found his element.

Ever hopeful that Chuck would return to his spiritual roots,

Connie often quipped, "Chuck, are you sure this is the way Dwight L. Moody started?" Connie had been content to remain with her husband, despite the discontent over not being able to have children and Chuck's insatiable pursuit of knowledge rather than trust. Connie dutifully did her best to help Chuck find that for which he was searching. More and more, though, she felt disconnected from his life. She winced when she thought about it. Her beloved Chuck was rapidly becoming one of the skeptical, cynical, intellectual snobs whose arrogance repulsed Connie. The one bright spot in her otherwise dreary existence was that Chuck had accepted an invitation from Dr. Henrietta Mears, Christian education director at Hollywood Presbyterian Church, to meet with a group of theologians and preachers gathering in California from around the world—and one of the speakers for the conference was Connie and Chuck's friend, Billy Graham.

Chapter Nineteen

FOREST HOME RETREAT CENTER, CALIFORNIA, AUGUST 1949

Almost immediately upon accepting the position of Christian education director for Hollywood's First Presbyterian Church in 1937, Dr. Henrietta Mears began searching for a suitable retreat center where she might periodically take the church's large youth group out of the city and away from the lights and frenzy of Hollywood. A feisty woman, known as well for her large, flamboyant, cockeyed hats decked with huge flowers as for her emphasis on biblical excellence, Dr. Mears sought a natural environment, a place where both teens and adults could relax and have fun, but where they could also sense the majesty of God's presence in the beauty of creation. She found just such a place in Forest Home, a resort in the San Bernardino Mountains, east of Los Angeles.

Forest Home had been the resort of choice in that area of California for years, and as Henrietta and some friends drove up the tree-shaded highway approaching the property, her first reaction was one of disappointment. The coffee shop, gas station, and lovely cabins in the circle by the fishpond looked inviting, as did the beautiful lodge and dining room. Overwhelmed by the grandeur of the setting, the magnificent stonework, and the expensive timbers, Mears wanted to turn around and go home. "I know we can't afford all this," she lamented.

But by 1937, in the years following the Depression, the owner had grown feeble and sickly, and his son feared that he would not have enough money to pay the taxes on the elegant property, estimated then at more than $350,000. They were willing to entertain all offers, even outrageous ones. Henrietta Mears and a group of Christian businessmen from California purchased the property for a mere $30,000! They formed a nonprofit corporation known as Forest Home, Inc., and dedicated the property to God, their stated goal that the hundreds of thousands of people they envisioned visiting the camp would find it a place where they could seek "to know Christ." Henrietta Mears expected people to make life-changing decisions at Forest Home Conference Center, and thousands did.

In 1949, Forest Home hosted a College Briefing Conference, a gathering designed to bring collegians together to discuss the Bible away from the hustle and bustle of campus. A gifted and highly respected Bible teacher herself, Henrietta Mears's class of college students taught at Hollywood Presbyterian Church had grown to more than five hundred students, many of whom would be attending the conference at Forest Home. At the same time, as was her custom, Dr. Mears invited some of the most outstanding biblical thinkers and speakers of the day to join them. At the '49 Conference, she planned for three keynote speakers: Dr. J. Edwin Orr, a PhD from Oxford University; Henrietta herself; and Billy Graham.

Billy had originally consented to come to Forest Home as a conferee only, rather than a speaker. Exhausted from his already busy speaking schedule, he had the added stress of trying to plan an evangelistic campaign in downtown Los Angeles, the largest citywide campaign Billy and his small staff had attempted to date. The first service was only weeks away, and Billy felt inadequately prepared, underfinanced, and deeply concerned about the overall effectiveness of the campaign. Nevertheless, despite his own problems, Billy consented to attend the conference, and Mears insisted that he be a part of the faculty.

She greeted him warmly when he arrived early for the conference that was scheduled to begin on Sunday and extend through the week. "Billy, how wonderful to see you!"

"Thank you, ma'am," he said as he handed her a bouquet of flowers, freshly purchased before making the trek up the mountain. "So good to see you as well."

"Oh, Billy. You are always thoughtful." She took the flowers from his hands. "Come inside, please."

Billy walked inside a lovely cottage at the Forest Home Conference Center and was immediately greeted by several colleagues and other guests who had been specially invited by Henrietta Mears to meet privately before the remainder of the conference attendees arrived.

Bob Evans, whom Billy had met at Wheaton, greeted Billy robustly. "Billy! Glad you made it." Bob steered Billy toward another distinguished gentleman, also named Evans—Dr. Louis Evans, the pastor of Hollywood Presbyterian Church. "Dr. Evans, Billy is one of ours, a Wheaton grad." Billy and Dr. Evans shook hands vigorously.

"Nice to meet you, Billy."

"My pleasure, sir. I've heard so much about you, Dr. Evans. I'll look forward to—"

Just then the cottage door swung open, banging against the doorstop, and Charles Templeton burst into the room, with his wife, Connie, barely holding on to his arm. Templeton wore a blue jacket with a Princeton emblem embroidered on the breast pocket. Swaggering across the room, the gregarious Charles immediately became the focus of attention, calling out names and greeting each person loudly.

Although surprised at Charles's flamboyant entrance, Billy was nonetheless glad to see his old friend. With Forest Home's reputation as a conservative, Christ-centered facility, and Henrietta Mears's track record for promoting only Bible-believing speakers, Billy was actually encouraged that Charles would attend the conference, especially in light of the last conversation he and Charles had shared prior to Chuck's departure for Princeton.

Templeton continued working his way around the room, making special note of each person. "Lewis! You are looking well. Robert! Good to see you!" Standing nearby the two Evans men, Billy looked toward Charles, waiting his turn to greet him.

Charles noticed Billy but turned his back on him to speak to someone else, as though Billy were not even standing there.

"Jack, I read your dissertation on neoorthodoxy and the Barth comparative study. Brilliant work!" Charles gushed.

Hurt deeply, Billy watched his friend mingle with other guests in the room. Chuck had yet to acknowledge that Billy was present. Connie, however, dragged along on the arm of the Princeton jacket, waved sweetly to Billy. She tilted her head, as though embarrassed.

Billy awkwardly waved back to her.

"Thank you, Charles. I'm afraid it raises more questions than it answers . . ." Billy heard the man reply to Templeton.

Determined to force Chuck to speak to him, Billy interrupted their conversation. "Chuck! It's good to see you," he said, as though Chuck had not been aware of his presence for the past few minutes.

Templeton pursed his lips, turned toward Billy, and tilted his head back, as if trying to take in Billy's frame. "Billy. Are you still speaking for God?"

Billy was caught off guard by his friend's caustic remark, clearly intended by Templeton to be derisive.

Billy sloughed it off with a nervous laugh, then said, "God's already spoken for Himself. I just testify about what His Word has meant to me—"

Templeton abruptly and rudely interrupted Billy. "Billy, Billy, the world has grown so much more complex in the last fifty years. People seeking the truth can no longer accept the simple rhetoric with which you were raised and still preach. When are you going to get that?" Templeton looked around the room to make sure everyone was listening before continuing to excoriate his friend. Satisfied that enough eyes and ears were trained in his direction, Charles looked haughtily at Billy and said, "That old-time religion—it's not good enough for me. It's not good enough for you either."

Billy looked back at his friend silently, thunderstruck by Templeton's audacity, deeply saddened by his spiritual arrogance, and crushed by Charles's betrayal of their friendship. At long last, Bob Evans intervened, "Hey, Chuck, go easy here!" He threw an arm around Templeton's shoulder, easing him away from Billy. "This is a reception, not a debate."

Billy stood watching as Chuck and Bob moved across the

floor, a few feet away from him. Connie smiled weakly as she trailed along behind, brushing a tear from her eye.

Billy had been so upset by Chuck's behavior, he hadn't noticed that his host, Henrietta Mears, had stepped up to his side. "Outspoken young man, isn't he?" she said with a sad smile. "Bless his heart."

Billy looked at Henrietta and nearly broke into a smile himself. He was from the South. He knew what Henrietta was implying.

Across the room, Templeton was still speaking much more loudly than necessary. "I'm doing him a big favor, Bob! People no longer accept the Bible as being divinely inspired. There are too many inconsistencies, lapses, lacunas. How could any of us presume that a document written by men is the sacrosanct, infallible, inalienable Word of God? *It's a fairy tale.*"

Billy couldn't help himself. He stepped back toward Charles. "More than two thousand years ago, the Scriptures prophesied that God would gather the Jewish people from the four corners of the earth and bring them back to their homeland—," Billy began, intending to state that the recent establishment of the renewed Jewish state of Israel was a fulfillment of prophecy—that they were the first generation since the year AD 70, when the Romans tore down the temple brick by brick, to see the nation of Israel back on the map. Billy never got that far, though, as Charles raised his powerful voice, interrupting again, and dominating the discussion.

"God didn't create the state of Israel, Billy. The UN did. After six million Jews, God's so-called chosen people, were gassed and burned in Hitler's ovens. Six million people, Billy! All of them praying to their God to be spared and not one prayer answered. Is that your loving God? Can you find Him in Auschwitz, Nagasaki, or Dresden? How could a loving God have condoned that?"

"Charles, you know better," Billy gently chastised him. "God didn't do that. Man did."

"Then God permitted it, didn't He? He didn't raise a finger to stop it. And you're out there preaching the good news! What good news, Billy?"

"The good news is that God so loved mankind that He gave His only Son, Jesus, so that . . ." Billy spoke like a man deflated, as though reality had poked holes in his idealism, and he didn't know what else to say, except that which he always said . . . and for some reason, it wasn't enough this time.

Templeton continued to rail against him. "Billy, I believe that Jesus was the purest example of all that is good in mankind. I believe that Jesus was the most influential teacher in the history of Western civilization, and I believe that Jesus was the most perfect moral being in the history of the world . . . but I do not believe he was the Son of God! He was the son of man! He said so himself."

The room fell silent as Charles pushed in front of Billy, raised up to his full athletic stature, and spoke so closely to Billy's face that Billy could feel Templeton's breath. "I feel sorry for you, Billy. What you call faith is truly the death of intellect. Your intellect." Templeton turned on his heel and left the room, purposely banging the door as he exited. Connie quickly gathered her purse and her wrap and hurried out behind him.

✂

The questions Charles posed were not new to Billy; he had pondered them many times himself. In recent months, especially in his role as a college president, he felt it incumbent upon himself to formulate answers to the questions that many of the Bible students at Northwestern might face, including Charles's favorite caveat, "How could a loving God allow such evil in the world?" Billy also tried his best to read widely among the better neoorthodox materials, such as those produced by Karl Barth and Reinhold Niebuhr, but their constant infusion of traditional theological terms with new, unfamiliar, and, in many cases, unbiblical meanings confused Billy and left him spiritually dry as dust.

Billy had little problem accepting the deity of Jesus Christ; neither did he doubt the resurrection of Christ or the validity of the gospel. But when it came to believing that the Bible was completely true, that it was the divinely inspired Word of God, Charles's questions were softballs compared to the curves Billy threw at himself. Could he accept all of the Bible as the Word of God and preach it with honesty, authority, and conviction if there were portions of the Scriptures that presented him with intellectual difficulties, dichotomies that he did not have the knowledge or wisdom to resolve?

As Billy had confessed to Charles, he recognized a distinct difference in the response of people—even unbelievers—when he not only based his statements on the Bible but actually quoted it. He had developed a habit of reminding his audiences, "The Bible says" this, or "The Bible says" that. He couldn't explain it, but he was convinced a power accompanied the quoting of the Scripture that could not be explained in mere human terms.

Moreover, evidence from modern archaeology was validating Billy's belief in the Bible, increasingly so every day. Since he made a practice of salting his sermons with current events, Billy had read the news of the recent discoveries near the Dead Sea. He noted with interest that in 1947, a Bedouin goatherd was out searching for some lost animals and had entered a cave in the cliffs near Qumran, about eight miles from Jericho. In the cave, the man found several jars, over two feet in height and about ten inches wide. Inside the jars were ancient leather scrolls wrapped in linen cloth. When the scrolls were examined, they were discovered to contain fragments of the Bible. More caves were explored, and more scrolls were found, most significantly, an intact copy of the Old Testament book of Isaiah, dating back to approximately 200 BC, including all of his predictions of the Messiah as the "suffering Servant." Liberal scholars had said for years that this book must have been pieced together by various authors shortly before—or possibly even after—the time of Jesus. The Dead Sea Scrolls proved otherwise. Although the war in the Middle East had delayed further discoveries from the area, it was clear that archaeology was confirming the historical accuracy of the ancient books.

Beyond that, Billy pondered the attitude of Jesus toward the Scriptures. Clearly, Jesus believed the Old Testament stories, and He even quoted some of those that Charles frequently mocked, such as Jonah and the whale and Noah and the ark. Jesus quoted at least twenty-four different books of the Old Testament and specifically stated that the Bible could be believed.

As far as Billy was concerned, if Jesus believed the Bible, quoted it, and attested to its veracity, why couldn't he?

ᗍᔕ

Still, Charles's needling of him rankled in Billy's mind all day long. He had been embarrassed and insulted by a friend—his best friend—in front of Henrietta Mears and her guests. Not exactly the most uplifting way to begin a weeklong conference in which he was considered an authority on the Bible in front of a group of

inquisitive collegians. Fortunately, Dr. Orr preached the opening
night of the conference. After the meeting, Billy asked Henrietta
if he could use her phone to call home.

"Of course, Billy," she said. "The phone is right over there on
the table by the wall. I'll give you some privacy."

"Thank you, Miss Mears," Billy responded as he sat down at
the table to place his collect telephone calls. Ordinarily, Billy's first
call was to Ruth and the children back in Montreat, but for some
reason, when the operator asked for the number he wished to call,
Billy gave her the number of his parents.

Billy's mother, Morrow Graham, answered the telephone and
accepted the collect charges for Billy's call from California to North
Carolina. She was surprised to hear from him, especially given the
lateness of the hour, North Carolina being three hours ahead of
California. "Billy, what's the matter? Is something wrong?" his
mother asked, instantly alert.

Billy's dad looked at the time and groused, "Is that Billy? Is
everything okay?" Morrow waved him off, indicating that she
would tell Frank as soon as she found out.

Billy's voice was despondent. "Momma, I no longer know
who I am," he said. "Everywhere I turn, I'm alone. I'm alone with
my doubts and questions. And . . ." His voice trailed off, and
Morrow thought that perhaps he had fallen asleep or hung up.

"Billy. Remember the time Bob Jones prophesied your failure?
Remember when Emily rejected you? Remember when you did
not know which direction to take?"

"I feel lost, Momma . . ."

Frank Graham rolled over and looked at Morrow. "You tell
that boy how expensive these long-distance—"

"Frank!" Morrow said his name in such a way that Frank

knew this was serious. He and Morrow exchanged a look. Frank nodded in understanding.

Morrow turned her attention back to her son. "Billy, God is with you. He will never leave you nor forsake you. He's promised you that, son. You know that, Billy. Call Ruth. She loves you, and she will be there for you. We will pray for you. I don't understand everything that is going on, but I know that God will show you the truth."

Frank moved close to Morrow and held out his hand. She clasped on to it tightly as she talked to Billy on the telephone.

"This one thing I do know: you *will* hear His voice again, and when you do, it will carry you for the rest of your life."

"Thank you, Momma," Billy said. "Pray for me."

"We will, Billy," his mother replied. "We surely will."

"Good night, Momma. I love you. And tell Daddy that I love him too. Don't worry about me. I'll be okay."

"Good night, son." Morrow Graham hung up the phone, and she and Frank slipped to their knees in prayer.

Meanwhile, Billy dialed zero for the long-distance operator once again. This time, he gave her his own home phone number.

The phone rang but twice before Ruth picked it up and groggily answered, "Hello?"

The operator, in her usual businesslike tone, rattled off, "I have a collect call from a Mr. Billy Graham. Will you accept the charges?"

"What? Why, yes, of course."

"Thank you; go ahead please," the operator said as she dropped off the call.

"Ruth!" Billy nearly cried into the telephone. "I wanted to hear your voice."

"How does it sound?" Ruth quipped.

"Oh, Ruth. You sound wonderful!" Billy said. "Real good, in fact." Billy took a deep breath. His normally clear, strong voice seemed weak. "But, Ruth, I've been thinking. Maybe we ought to go back to the farm. Maybe I'm not cut out for this."

Ruth quickly realized that her husband was having another serious bout with doubt. It was not a time for frivolity or mischievous banter. She sat up in the bed. "Billy, I love you. More than I ever thought it was possible to love any man."

For a long moment, Billy remained silent. When he finally spoke, he did so with passion and intensity. "And I love you, and I miss you. And I want to come home."

Ruth continued her thought, speaking at the same time as Billy. "I'm glad you wanted to hear my voice. But it's not my voice you need to hear tonight."

Billy stared at the phone in his hand. Ruth was right. This was not between him and his wife; it was not between him and Chuck; it was between Billy and his God.

೧

For the next several days at Forest Home, Billy went through the motions of ministry, but with no further insight as to how he should answer his friend's objections to the Bible and no fresh assurance to assuage his own doubts. He spoke each morning to the collegians, and for all his personal conflict, proved to be quite effective—especially when he emphasized God's Word as the absolute truth, the standard for judging right and wrong in this life, and the basis on which all other decisions could be made. The collegians responded enthusiastically when Billy said, "The Bible says . . ." which he did frequently.

Billy took advantage of the time when he was not speaking or talking informally with the college students to seek an end to the impasse in his own spiritual life. He spoke often and candidly with Dr. Henrietta Mears and with Dr. Orr, admitting to them the difficult issues with which he was struggling. Both of them had brilliant minds—Henrietta, a former high school chemistry teacher, and Edwin Orr, an Oxford professor who was one of the world's leading authorities on the history of religious revivals—yet both had a deep confidence in the integrity of the Scriptures, as well as a marvelous grasp of modern scholarship and biblical criticism. Moreover, Dr. Mears and Dr. Orr both laid great emphasis on complete surrender to God and the infilling of His Holy Spirit as essential elements to victorious Christian living. The three of them prayed together frequently as the week progressed, asking God to bring the matter in Billy's heart and mind to some form of resolution.

One evening after dinner, Billy went back alone to his own cabin to read again some of the scriptures that he could recall emphasizing the power and reliability of God's Word. Searching through his Bible, he found numerous instances in which God's Word proved authoritative and true when all other sources of wisdom fell short.

Yet as the night wore on, Billy's heart and mind became even more burdened. The Los Angeles campaign loomed largely in his thoughts. Members of the Christian Businessmen's Committee of Greater Los Angeles had worked themselves almost to exhaustion trying to put together the evangelistic meetings, which were to be held in a Ringling Brothers circus tent set up especially for the occasion on a parking lot. The tent was huge, supposedly holding as many as six thousand people. Billy worried whether enough people would attend to fill the first few rows. He had implored the committee to raise more money for advertising, including the distribution of posters and flyers all over the city. But resources were limited, and everything about the campaign required enormous amounts of money, most of which had to be raised before the campaign could open. As Billy left Minneapolis for California to attend the conference at Forest Home, that concern weighed heavily on his heart and mind.

And what if people did come? What would he tell them? That he wasn't quite sure, but that he *thought* the Bible was God's Word? That it *might* be the definitive source for wisdom and direction in a person's life? That perhaps it may include a possible means of forgiveness and salvation? Maybe it was a road map to heaven, one of many possible truths, as Charles had taken to regarding the Book.

No, that would never do. Billy had to have an answer for himself. If he could not trust the Bible, he would quit preaching. He would resign as president of Northwestern, resign from the Youth for Christ evangelistic staff, disband his own fledgling evangelistic association, and go back into another line of work.

As Billy grappled with these issues, he decided to take a walk. It was a clear, cool night in the San Bernardino Mountains, with the moon peaking over the mountaintop, brightly shining above the treetops and casting large shadows below as Billy made his way to a trail that ran into the woods and farther up the mountainside. Billy doubted that he would be able to see the words in the shadowy light, but he carried his Bible with him anyway. Far from the city of Los Angeles, and now far from the laughter and jovial voices he had heard emanating from the gathering of collegians at the conference center, the only sounds Billy heard now were songs of the cicadas, the snapping of twigs beneath his feet, or the occasional hoot of an owl out searching for a late-night snack. Although he didn't know it at the time, Billy was near a spot where, more than seventy years earlier, on May 30, 1876, a group of fourteen eminent California citizens, led by then state treasurer Truman Reeves, had stood praying, dedicating the mountain "to the service of the Lord."

In that same vicinity, Henrietta Mears had a practice of closing every conference at Forest Home with a huge bonfire in a white-stone amphitheater that she called Victory Circle. As the fire blazed, young men and women stepped out one by one to toss a small piece of wood or a stick into the fire, publicly symbolizing that they had made a decision to wholeheartedly follow Jesus Christ. Thousands of young men and women made serious, life-changing commitments on that mountain; some made commitments that changed the world.

There was no bonfire that night, so for a while, Billy wandered along the forest trail, alone with his thoughts, desperate for God, hoping to sense His presence in the natural setting around him—surrounded by tall trees swaying in the gentle breeze, the sweet scent of the pine trees wafting through the air, and soft moonlight illuminating the path. Billy ambled farther into the woods until he spotted a large tree stump, quite similar to the one that had been in his own backyard as he was growing up. He trudged over to it; placed his Bible on the stump, letting the pages fall open as he dropped to his knees in front of it; and began to pray. He prayed fervently and passionately, speaking aloud to God, sometimes with his eyes wide open, sometimes with his eyes tightly closed, beads of perspiration forming on his forehead, losing all track of time, calling out to God as though he were imploring a close friend from whom he desperately needed help.

Had Billy been able to see beyond the thin veil that separates this world from the spirit world, he would no doubt have been surprised and possibly terrified at the spiritual battle being waged in the heavenlies all around him. Lucifer, also known as the accuser of the brethren, the longstanding enemy of Yahweh, and now the personal enemy of Billy's soul, was bidding high for him that night, commanding his minions to do everything within their power—which allowed for significant oppression—to divert Billy Graham from the destiny God had planned for him. Billy himself was yet oblivious to much of that master plan, but the accuser, through six thousand years of cataloged experience, could see and ascertain what was coming. It was clear to him, if not to mere mortals, that the Holy One of Israel had something special in mind for the young evangelist, that because of his "heart after God," his sincere dedication, and his willingness to completely pour out his life to God, he had within him the potential to have as much influence or more in spreading the gospel than any human being who had ever previously walked the earth. Lucifer and his cohorts were determined to prevent that from happening.

Lucifer knew, too, what many immature Christians fail to understand: that a successful journey with God involves daily choices. Certainly, long before Billy's birth, God had laid out a path for Billy's life, but He had not created Billy as a mindless automaton. Neither was the calling on his life sacrosanct; at any point, Billy could choose which way he would go—whether to align himself with God's plan or to veer off in his own direction. Lucifer's goal was to continually present options other than the straight and narrow path, opportunities that might look more desirable, more attractive, or less demanding to Billy than those offered by his heavenly Father. Moreover, after eons of practice,

Lucifer was a master at pushing a person's psychological buttons. He expertly devised and perfected, by trial and error, myriad temptations to be uniquely applicable and to appeal most effectively to the deficiencies in a person's character, so he might exploit them for his evil purposes. In every case, Lucifer knew that it all came down to the question of faith. If he could diminish or extinguish the flame of faith, he would carry the day in the battle for the ultimate prize: the soul.

Yet Lucifer knew his own place, that he was not equal with God; indeed, he was nothing more than a created being—one that had deliberately chosen to rebel against God, had suffered the consequences of those decisions, and in the process had influenced a large number of other created beings to follow his disastrous choices. More than most earthlings realized, Lucifer chafed at his own limitations, like a wild animal tethered by a heavy-linked chain, painfully aware that no matter how he stalked and howled, his vaunted, omnipresent, omnipotent strength was a sham; he could only stretch so far and do so much. Lucifer knew that he could not force Billy to make wrong choices, that his only power against Billy was to make every scheming effort to tempt him away from the infallibility of the Book. Yet, even if Lucifer failed at his highest goal, there remained other options.

He could surely tempt Billy to compromise, if not to break away from his faith, perhaps simply to walk away from his calling; or possibly he could lure Billy to acquiesce to the most seductive of stratagems—to live in a lesser sphere of influence than what the Father had in mind for him. After all, what could be wrong with that? Billy would make a fine pastor of a local church, a wonderful missionary, or perhaps an outstanding Sunday school teacher. Any distraction or diversion would do, actually, and Lucifer would be delighted to enhance the opportunity if it could somehow thwart the great purposes the Father had planned for Billy.

Up until now, Billy's life had been marked by a series of tests, some deceptively designed by the enemy to draw Billy off the path; others provided by the heavenly Father to examine Billy and to allow him to examine himself, to help him recognize his deepest needs, to teach him to trust, to prepare him for the next level of influence. For Billy, who could not see the source of these tests, the line between temptation and testing was often obscured.

Nevertheless, much to Lucifer's chagrin, Billy repeatedly passed the tests. Not that he always performed perfectly or never tasted failure, but like a high jumper who throws his heart over the pole, knowing that his body will follow, Billy continued to throw his head and heart over the line between faith and reason, believing that as he did so, God would guide his steps and supply whatever understanding and knowledge he needed. Despite the obstacles—whether it was discouragement heaped on him by his rugged, austere father; rejection by Emily; repeated reminders of his own inadequacies; Dr. Bob Jones's blatant predictions of failure; or intellectual humiliation by Charles Templeton—Billy had consistently made good choices, based on his faith in God and his willingness to obey God's Word. But now, the veracity of God's Word, Billy's very foundation for living, had been challenged in such a way that it shook Billy, and he could feel himself teetering like one of the tall trees in the California forest, tipping, nearly ready to topple over as the ax wielded by a woodsman who looked a lot like Charles Templeton whaled away at the base of the trunk.

The enemy, too, recognized that he finally had Billy on the run, that Templeton's caustic remarks had gotten to him, and that the wounds of a friend sliced much deeper than snide comments from critics. Billy had admitted during his phone call to Ruth that he was on the verge of giving up and going back to working the farm. That's all Lucifer's forces needed to hear. They launched an even stronger barrage of doubt-inducing poison-tipped arrows aimed first at Billy's heart, and then at his mind.

No wonder Billy struggled in prayer. All available battalions of hellish fiends were staked out on the ground and in the air around him. Though invisible to his naked eyes, Billy sensed the presence of the enemy. He knew he had to pray again, and as he did, angelic protectors moved between Billy and the opposing forces.

Indeed, as Billy prayed, all of heaven came to attention. More angels were dispatched from the throne of grace to thwart the attack of the enemy forces. The Spirit of God who resided within Billy came alongside him to help, protect, and empower him. Other saints and celestial beings gathered on heaven's borders, overlooking the earth, a great cloud of witnesses acknowledging the power of faith, urging Billy onward, taking his name before the eternal Ancient of Days. Yet for all their intercession, they were powerless to do anything else at that point but to keep the demonic forces at bay and to wait and see what Billy would choose.

The cosmic battle raged on, with the angelic heavenly forces as well as the demonic legions from hell realizing more and more that Billy had not merely been called; he had been chosen before the foundations of the earth to take the gospel in some unique way to the world.

Billy's heart pounded in his chest; his face glistened with perspiration mixed with tears, as he persevered in prayer, refusing to let go of God until he received an answer. Besides fending off the onslaught from the enemy, Billy seemed, like Jacob of old, to be in a wrestling match with God as well, embroiled in a battle to maintain his faith and his calling and to secure God's blessing. Although Billy had no idea at the time that God's plans for him would make him a modern-day apostle, taking him to far-reaching capitals of the world, preaching to kings and presidents as well as to the common folk, the enemy recognized that potential and knew that hell's only hope was for Billy to squander away his calling by willfully making wrong decisions. All that and more was on the line as Billy struggled in prayer.

Billy remembered from his study of the Bible that Jesus patiently tolerated His disciples' questions, even their sometimes foolish lack of understanding regarding who He was, why He did the things He did, and what motivated and empowered Him. And he also knew that Jesus had strongly rebuked His disciples for their unbelief and lack of genuine faith. Billy did not wish to receive a similar rebuke, so he persisted in prayer, struggling to keep his doubts from turning into unbelief, while honestly expressing the cries of his heart.

Recognizing that the scale might possibly be tipping toward heaven, Lucifer pulled out the most lethal weapon in his arsenal. He carefully surveyed the battle status and found a crack in Billy's armor, opened by Billy's own doubts. The deceiver duped one of heaven's guards into allowing him brief access to Billy, and he fired, sending Charles Templeton's searing comment into Billy's mind: *You are committing intellectual suicide, and you know it!*

Lucifer hastily retreated to a safer location, where he could watch the delicious end play out. The accuser understood well that, like Charles Templeton, Billy was a man of honor and integrity, and he could not preach what he did not sincerely believe. Templeton had succumbed to the intellectual barrage against his faith, and now, with renewed effort, the forces of hell were thrusting that same charge against Billy Graham.

The enemy had somehow ascertained what was at stake; they recognized all too well that the man on his knees in front of the Bible on the stump could be one of heaven's greatest champions in the making. They had witnessed great men and women in history who had exercised their faith in God and had risen to have an influence for brief periods of time. Presidents served a mere four to eight years, and even the best of them could be easily discredited one way or another; godly kings, few of them that there were, had but limited influence. But this man, the guileless fool on his knees, he was dangerous. He could influence a generation, possibly two, three, or four. He might influence eternity. He had to be stopped.

Billy reeled under the intense oppression that attempted to infect and overpower him through the piercing blow to his faith. Kneeling at the tree stump, clutching the sides so tenaciously that his fingernails dug into the tree bark, he seemed to be hanging on only by the tiniest thread of hope as Templeton's words taunted him incessantly.

From his vantage point, Lucifer raised up to his full stature and gazed on the crumbling man on the ground. A devious smirk crossed his face; he had seen many strong men and women at this point. Innumerable others had succumbed much earlier, unwilling or unable to go further with God, acquiescing even though the way of escape stood open before them, and the power to step through it had been purchased at such an enormous price and was freely available to all who would appropriate it.

Few did.

Over the course of recorded human history, millions more had backed away than had pressed on with God. Only a few had dared to trust God wholeheartedly and live by faith. Lucifer winced as he thought of how effectively those few had influenced the world for good. He hated to lose, and he took malevolent comfort in knowing that statistically speaking, he rarely did.

The accuser smugly squared his frame, openly gloating over his work; he had delivered the piercing blow to Billy, and he was certain it had struck its target with full, deadly impact. Lucifer repressed a fiendish laugh as his brilliant mind recalled thousands of cases in which he had lured good men and women to this identical crucible, as they had tried to reconcile the seemingly incompatible elements of rationality and genuine faith. They were good men and women who never went on to achieve the great things they were designed to do, but, instead, because they allowed their doubts to solidify into disbelief, the burden dragged them down; they settled into a spiritual quagmire that slowly but surely smothered their destiny. Templeton was right where the enemy wanted him, and Lucifer was certain that Graham was about to follow him.

But wait. The nearly defeated foe was at the end of his rope. The perspiration, the tears, the pounding heart continued, but something else was happening. A cosmic hush settled over the cloud of witnesses in heaven and the inhabitants of hell. Everyone waited and watched in anticipation. This was pivotal. Nobody else could make the decision but Billy. Which way would he go? All of heaven rose in hope; all of hell squirmed grotesquely. Lucifer was one of the first to see what was coming, and he roared in disbelief. Whatever color Lucifer possessed drained from his being as he heard Billy cry out to God.

"Charles put me to the test, Lord." Billy shook his head and turned his face toward the sky as he spoke. "And I had nothing."

Somehow, admitting his own spiritual poverty seemed to open Billy's heart and mind even further. A breeze rustled the trees around him. He continued talking to God. "If You didn't want me to preach, why did You let me believe? And if You want me to believe, why can't You just give me some proof?"

Billy picked up the Bible and raised it toward the sky. "Oh, God, there are many things in this book that I don't understand. There are questions in this book that I just can't answer. There are some areas that don't seem to correlate with modern science. So give me something. Anything!" Billy pleaded, breathing heavily. "Where are You?" he railed at God. Billy slapped down his Bible on the top of the tree stump.

A sound similar to a clap of thunder shook the air, and a strong wind swept over Billy, rustling the pages of his Bible. Suddenly a collage of images streaked through Billy's mind. He saw his mother and heard her loving voice reminding him, "Jesus will never leave you nor forsake you." He saw his father and the group of five men gathered around the stump, praying for God to raise an ambassador to take the gospel to the world. He heard his loving wife, Ruth, saying, "He will speak to you again." Billy looked up, partly in surprise, yet it was more than surprise. He had an expression of awe on his face.

"I understand, Lord!" He looked back at the Bible. "You said in Your Word that the just shall live by *faith*." Billy looked skyward. "I see it, Lord. I accept it. I believe it—by faith."

Billy breathed heavily as his doubts seemed to be lifted off his shoulders. Although he could not see it happening, the demonic forces assailing him began to splinter and recede before the angelic host around Billy. Back. Back. Forced to retreat, they stumbled, fell, and eventually fled in terror. The last to leave was Lucifer himself, tasting once again the blood in his mouth, the same he tasted when the Lamb of God had crushed his head nearly two thousand years earlier. Reminded afresh that he was nothing more than a defeated foe, Lucifer whirled away from Billy and in an instant was gone.

Billy picked up his Bible again, gazing at it in wonder. "I am going to accept this book by faith," he prayed aloud. "I accept this book as Your infallible Word, by faith. It's beyond reason; because the Bible says, 'Take this by faith.' The righteous shall live *by faith*." Billy bowed his head. "Oh, thank You, Lord. Thank You!"

As Billy rose from the ground that night, his eyes stung with tears; not tears of remorse, but tears of sheer joy. His clothes were rumpled and soaked with perspiration, as though he had been in a wrestling match—which indeed he had, perhaps even more so than he knew at the time. Billy couldn't have cared less about his clothes. He was elated! He sensed God's presence in his life as he had not known in several months, maybe even longer. He still had many questions, but he had stepped across a line; in a simple yet enormously profound step of faith, he had crossed once and for all from doubting to believing. For the remainder of his life, Billy would regard this night as the turning point, when a major spiritual battle had been fought in his heart, mind, and soul . . . and he had won.

Regarding his trust in the infallibility and authority of God's Word, Billy later stated emphatically, "From that moment on, I can tell you before God, I've never had a doubt. And when I quote the Scripture, I know that I am quoting the Living Word of God. It has power. And from that moment on, my ministry changed, because I could speak with authority. I knew that the Bible was God's Word, and I knew it would not return void."[1]

---

1. Excerpted from an interview with Wayne Shepherd, WMBI Radio, Moody Bible Institute Spiritual Emphasis Week, Torrey–Gray Auditorium; Chicago, IL, November 13, 1973.

Whatever happened on that mountain, other people were quick to notice. Henrietta Mears was one of the first. "I did not know what had happened, but there was an authority, a sureness, a fire in his spirit that hadn't been there when he first arrived."[2]

Indeed, Billy spoke with a new confidence as he boldly proclaimed the gospel. At his very next seminar session the following day, Billy's words to the collegians conveyed an unusually strong passion. When he challenged the audience to dedicate their lives to Christ, more than four hundred people responded. Nothing in Billy's life or ministry would ever be the same.

ᏦᎧ

MONTREAT, NORTH CAROLINA, 1949

It was a long trip from California to North Carolina, but Billy wanted to go home before he went back to Northwestern to prepare for the fall semester. Ruth saw him coming and ran to greet him as he approached the house, carrying his suit bag. Billy dropped his belongings and swept Ruth off the ground into his arms.

"I'm back," Billy said.

It was all he needed to say. "Oh, Billy . . ." Ruth's tears of joy were already soaking the shoulder of his shirt.

Billy wasn't certain where his next trip would be, whether a return to Northwestern or back to Los Angeles to help do pre-campaign publicity. At present no publicity had been scheduled, because the Los Angeles media were not greatly interested in

---

2. Earl O. Roe, ed., *Dream Big: The Henrietta Mears Story* (Ventura, CA: Regal Books, 1990), 303.

talking with Billy, let alone talking about the upcoming campaign, and that was a problem.

Billy had urged the businessmen who called themselves "Christ for Greater Los Angeles" to think bigger in terms of their advertising budget. Billy was convinced that to do the campaign right, they needed about twenty-five thousand dollars. The committee had raised only seven thousand. The group had hosted other evangelistic efforts on even less money, and now they were asking Billy to come and do the preaching and to bring along George Beverly Shea as the featured soloist and Cliff Barrows as the choir director. Billy wasn't worried about raising more money for Cliff, Bev, or himself; but he knew that if the citywide campaign was to have long-lasting effects on Los Angeles, the people of L.A. had to know that something was indeed going on down there at the corner of Washington and Hill Streets, where the committee planned to set up the large circus tent. They had to get the word out. Otherwise, the entire effort would be in vain.

Back and forth the correspondence flew between Billy and the campaign organizers in California. The committee had already conceded on two important issues at Billy's request. One, they had broadened their efforts to gain the support of the local churches in the Los Angeles area. Billy felt this was important because the local churches could take ownership of the evangelistic effort, making it their own, encouraging their own people to attend and inviting nonbelievers. Billy knew, too, from his work with Youth for Christ that one of the key elements in helping new believers or people who had made fresh commitments to God was to involve them in some sort of "follow-up" program, in which they could hear good, solid, biblical preaching, where they could read and study the Bible and learn to pray for themselves, and where they could enjoy the company of other believers who could help them grow stronger in their new Christian faith. Billy knew that the best place for that to happen was in connection with local churches and their pastors. He held little interest in building a great name for the Billy Graham team if it could not help build the local churches. This inclusion and involvement of the local churches was to become a hallmark of Billy's ministry.

The second concession made by the Los Angeles committee was agreeing to set up a larger-than-necessary tent. Billy assured them that in his experience, the crowds normally increased rather than decreased as the campaign went along. But the third request—that of investing more money in advertising and promotion of the campaign—remained sticky.

Finally, although it pained him to do so, Billy wrote a letter to the Los Angeles hosting committee, telling them that he and his team would be forced to cancel the engagement if the organizers couldn't see the necessity to step out in faith and take the added financial risk required to promote the campaign. Billy poured out his heart in a letter to the committee: "I'm convinced," he wrote, "that if a revival could break out in the city of Los Angeles, it would have repercussions around the world. Let's not stop at anything to make this the meeting that God could use as a spark to send a flame of revival through the nation. Your responsibilities are tremendous. Let's go forward by prayer."[3]

Billy sent the letter off, praying that it would be received in the spirit in which he sent it—one with a desire to see Los Angeles touched by God.

---

3. Billy Graham, *Just as I Am* (New York: Harper Collins, 1997), 145.

❧

After a short stay at home, Billy headed back to Northwestern. The school was already bustling with activity in anticipation of the students' return to campus early in September. Billy bounded into the office, still feeling refreshed and relaxed from his pivotal time at Forest Home. Luverne was waiting for him with her usual stack of pink messages. T. W. was in the office too. He handed Billy a letter, already opened.

"Los Angeles called back," he said straightforwardly, with no hint of emotion.

"Oh really?" Billy's cheerful, relaxed countenance suddenly turned concerned, fearful, almost intimidated. "What did they say?"

T. W. broke into a wide smile. "They raised the twenty-five thousand. What do I tell them?"

"Tell them we'll be there!" Billy said with a whoop.

Chapter Twenty

TORONTO, 2001

The immaculately dressed, elderly gentleman arrived at Pearson International Airport in Toronto, Canada, and along with his long-time travel companion, made his way to the waiting car in the frigid winter of 2001. Once settled inside the car, he unbuttoned his dark topcoat and leaned back on the automobile's headrest. The driver glanced in the mirror at the octogenarian in his rear seat, noting that the distinguished, white-haired gentleman had already closed his eyes. The man's companion nodded to the driver, who pulled the vehicle into traffic and headed toward the hospital.

"It's just a short ride," the driver said. "I'll have you there in no time at all."

"Thank you," the aged gentleman answered in a raspy but friendly voice, without opening his eyes. "We may not have much time left." He settled back in the seat, eyes still closed, resting, or perhaps praying.

❦

TEMPLETON'S HOSPITAL ROOM, 2001

Charles Templeton fidgeted nervously as he recalled Billy Graham's Los Angeles campaign. Even though he and Billy had been at odds on their theology, Charles had consented to speak for a "booster dinner" held by the Christian Businessmen's Committee of Greater Los Angeles in July, preceding the campaign, hoping to drum up some enthusiasm for the proposed evangelistic series in the fall. Charles knew that he had not done his old friend any favors by telling them that he and Billy were taking two different roads. For years after the Forest Home debacle, Templeton would insist that he had been misunderstood, that his cutting remarks, which had seared into Billy's soul, had been garbled in the retelling. No matter. God used them for good, much to Templeton's added chagrin.

Deborah Matthews leaned in closely to Templeton, so close that he could smell the sensuous scent of her perfume. She laid her hand on Templeton's forearm as she spoke. "I know you are tired, sir, but just a few more questions, if you don't mind."

"Mind? I don't mind at all," Templeton replied, his imagination as well as his attention piqued, as Deborah hoped they might be.

Deborah leaned back in her chair and crossed her legs, looking surprisingly relaxed as she balanced a clipboard on her thigh. "Tell us some more about that first Graham crusade in Los Angeles. Why was it such a big event?"

"Big event?" Templeton mimicked her. "It was nothing of the sort . . . at least not in its initial form. In fact, the press labeled it a *none*vent because it was just that—a nonevent, and that's what I've been trying to tell you. Billy Graham was a nonevent."

Deborah uncrossed her legs and leaned in toward Templeton

again. "Then *how* do you explain what happened in Los Angeles?"
she asked airily.

Templeton looked at her for a long moment, as though trying
to decide if she really wanted to know, and if he really wanted to
tell her. Finally he spoke quietly. "The only way I can rationally
explain Billy's success is . . ." His voice increased in volume and
intensity as he said, "*Puff Graham!*"

"'Puff Graham'? You've said that once before. What does it
mean?"

"The Los Angeles campaign was languishing . . . Oh, the
people were coming, all right. Most small auditoriums or churches
would have been packed. About three thousand people per night
were showing up at the Los Angeles campaign, but three thousand
in a tent that could hold six thousand? A drop in the bucket,"
Templeton chortled, and then grew serious again. "And then it
happened; everything exploded. Out of nowhere, all of a sudden,
Jane Russell, the movie star, appears at Henrietta Mears's Beverly
Hills home to listen to Billy talking to some Hollywood celebrity
types . . . and she wants to be saved! Of all things!"

Templeton appeared agitated again and began talking to himself
and looking around the room. At least it seemed as much to Deborah
and her film crew. They could not see what Templeton was seeing:
demons taunting him, mocking him, laughing at him hideously. The
demons swirled around Templeton's head, pummeling his mind with
images of Auschwitz; of mangled, murdered bodies; of lice-infested,
nearly starved to death naked prisoners; of dead men, women, and
children stacked ignominiously in open, common pits for burial.

"Go away!" Templeton bellowed, swatting at the air. "Stop
bothering me! *Get out!*" he roared. Templeton turned his face away
from the camera and stared toward the wall.

His outburst brought his nurse to the doorway of his hospital room. She looked at Templeton, then at Deborah, and rolled her fingers as if to say, *Wrap it up.*

Deborah nodded, then quickly turned back to Templeton. "What is it, sir? What's the matter?" She leaned close to Templeton and almost whispered, "What do you see?"

Templeton's eyes darted around the room. He started to speak . . . and then caught himself. He fanned his hand back and forth in front of his face. "Nothing, nothing. I'm fine now. Just tired. I'm an old man, you know . . . and this is a lot of stress on me. I don't need this."

Deborah feared losing him before the climax. "All right, all right," she said smoothly, nodding. "All right. Let's just take a deep breath. This story is important; let's finish this right."

Templeton leaned toward Deborah and stretched his neck to the side of her face as though he were going to whisper in her ear. "You're not leaving, are you?" he asked, almost fearfully.

Deborah wasn't certain whether he was talking to her or to someone else . . .

Even with his mind darkened by the Alzheimer's disease, Templeton remembered the Los Angeles campaign so very well. He smiled slightly as he recalled Billy even referring to him in one of his sermons—obtusely, of course . . .

ఆ

LOS ANGELES, 1949

Billy Graham stood on a 150-foot platform at one end of the circus tent. Directly behind the pulpit rose a twenty-foot-high and twenty-foot-wide replica of an open Bible. Although the Bible had been erected by the Christ for Los Angeles team, Billy took it as a silent testimony to his own renewed confidence in the Book as the Word of God. Following his experience at Forest Home a few weeks earlier, Billy was convinced that the Bible was unlike any other book ever written. It was the divinely inspired Word of God, and when it was taught and preached in the power of God's Holy Spirit, people's lives could be changed.

Billy leaned his tall frame over the pulpit, reading the Scripture with his hands folded behind his back. After his customary thanks and a quick joke, he pressed into his message, growing more intense as he went along. Billy preached with a new power and fervor, rising often to his tiptoes as he delivered the message, sometimes pacing the large platform, clenching his fists as he spoke, often stabbing his finger into the air as if pointing at every person in the tent, including those farthest away from him, even people sitting or standing outside the tent flaps.

Always, his message centered on Jesus Christ and how a person could know Him, how a person *must* know Him to be saved—saved from sin, saved from self, saved from satanic delusions, but more important, saved to enjoy a relationship with God during this life and throughout eternity. Billy's voice, ever strong and clear, seemed imbued with a new power, even as he recounted some of Charles Templeton's conversations with him. "Now, I have a friend, a dear friend," Billy said, purposely emphasizing the word *friend,* "who told me Jesus was a man, nothing but a man."

Billy paused and looked around at the faces in the crowd. "Well, He was a man; He was human. Jesus was not a white man; He was not a black man; He came from that part of the world that touches Africa and Asia and Europe, and He probably had brown skin." He let those words sink in, knowing that while they were obvious to many of his listeners, to some who insisted on their own preconceived notions of Jesus, they would be considered quite radical.

"Christianity," Billy went on, "is not a white man's religion, and don't let anybody ever tell you that it's white or black. So who was this unusual man who has marched across history? Who can explain Him? There's never been anybody like Him. Even my good friend who is an atheist will tell you that!" Billy paused again. Referring to his friend as an atheist felt odd to Billy—the term itself sticking in his throat the way a newly divorced person struggles when referring for the first time to his or her former spouse. It wasn't supposed to be this way. The word stung like sea water in an open wound.

Billy quickly brought the focus back to Jesus. "He had a ministry of only three years, and yet two thousand years later, millions upon millions on every continent bow down and worship Him. Why? How is that possible?

"Because He was sent to redeem us. He hung on the cross to redeem us, and on that cross, He touched the finger of God with one hand, and with the other hand He reached out and took *your* hand—and in that moment, He reconciled God and man."

The amazing truth of his message stunned even Billy, as he stopped again, momentarily allowing his words to move from the brain down into the heart. He looked at the crowd and sensed that they were ready to take action on what they had heard. "I'm asking you tonight to commit your life to Him," Billy said straightforwardly. "It won't be easy. It's tough; it's hard; there are those who will mock you, but there is a joy and a peace and a satisfaction in living that kind of a life, in following Christ, a serenity that fills the emptiness that is in your heart. And once you have it"—his voice rose in pitch and intensity—"you know where you are going.

And you know where you've come from, and you know what life is all about; you know why you're here, and you know where you're going when you die." Billy put his hands together as though he were praying. "Now I'm going to ask you to get up out of your seat, wherever you are, and stand in front of this platform and say by coming, 'I know that I am a sinner. I want to receive Christ into my heart; I want my sins forgiven. I want to know that I am going to heaven. I want a new life, and I want it to begin tonight. I want it to begin right here, right now.'"

Billy scanned the audience again, almost as though he could tell who in the crowd was being deeply affected by his words, but he never knew for sure. That part of the message was where the Spirit of God took over; Billy knew that his job was to present the Word clearly, simply, so people could understand.

"You may be saying, 'I want that. I want that kind of new life to begin right now.' And it can. It doesn't matter if you're a movie star or the biggest drunk on the streets of Los Angeles. God is waiting for you right now."

Billy spread his arms wide as he stepped to the side of the pulpit and extended the invitation for those seeking to meet Jesus Christ, as well as those in need of spiritual help, to come forward, to the front of the tent, where counselors were already gathering, ready to assist and pray with those who responded.

"Come!" Billy urged. "You, come!"

And people did. Not many at first, but more as the days of the campaign went on.

❦

One night Billy looked out into the sea of faces and saw a man he recognized, one whom many Californians recognized too, at least by voice. Stuart Hamblen was a tremendously popular radio personality whose show was heard up and down the West Coast. A tall, strong Texan and a genuine cowboy, Stuart was rough, loud, and hard as nails, spiritually as well as physically. Billy had met Stuart at the home of Henrietta Mears just prior to the beginning of the evangelistic campaign. Stuart and Billy hit it off immediately, and Stuart had jokingly told him then that Billy's tent would be filled if Stuart endorsed him.

Of course Billy invited Stuart to attend. In return, Stuart extended an invitation for Billy to be a guest on his radio show. At the time, most evangelists rarely appeared on secular media programs, and it was risky for Billy to do so too. After all, Stuart was known as a heavy drinker, a gambler, and a rather salty, rough-talking character. Billy felt that since Jesus set the precedent by dining in the homes of tax collectors and sinners, he could at least appear on Stuart's program.

Billy did the show, and Stuart proved well behaved. He even surprised Billy by encouraging the listeners to attend the tent meetings. "Go on down to Billy Graham's tent and hear the preaching," Stuart said. Then he really shocked Billy and probably many of his listeners as well. "I'll be there too."

True to his word, Stuart showed up at the tent, but the first night he attended, Billy preached hard about sin, and Stuart didn't care for what he heard. He angrily stalked out of the tent.

The next few nights, Stuart avoided the campaign, but he couldn't keep from talking about it, often derisively, on his radio show. Before long, Stuart was back at the tent. But then the next day, he would rail and rant about what a joke it was. Day after day, Hamblen irreverently mocked the tent revival, going out each evening to load up on fresh material. His radio listeners loved it.

But for all his rough talk and rugged exterior, something was happening on the inside of Stuart Hamblen. Billy's messages were getting through, even though on another night Stuart stormed out, shaking his fists at Billy.

But the next evening, he was back.

Then one night, long after the meeting was over, Billy received a phone call in his room at Langham Hotel. Sleepily, he looked at his watch; it was four thirty in the morning, and Stuart Hamblen was on the line—in tears, begging to see Billy. After rousing Ruth, Billy called Grady Wilson and his wife, Wilma, asking them to come immediately to pray while Stuart was en route.

Soon Stuart and his wife, Suzy—who had been praying for Stuart for some time—knocked on Billy's door. They talked for a while and then prayed together, and the rough-and-tough cowboy asked God to forgive him of his sins, as he put his trust in Jesus Christ and made up his mind to follow Him.

Stuart became a true believer. He later wrote a song about his experience following a conversation he had with noted film star John Wayne. The song was called "It Is No Secret (What God Can Do)," and it quickly became one of George Beverly Shea's most requested numbers. Not long afterward, Stuart wrote another song describing his former life of sin and his new life that had been reshaped by God. "This Ole House," which became a hit on secular radio, has been recorded hundreds of times by artists of almost every musical genre.

The following week Hamblen spoke openly and unabashedly about his conversion to anyone who would listen—and millions did, as Stuart told the entire story on his radio show, telling people specifically how Jesus Christ had changed his life. Suddenly people in California were talking not only about Stuart but also about that evangelist who had introduced him to Christ, the same one who was still in town, conducting services outdoors under a circus tent. The tent began to fill up more and more each night.

One night, when Billy arrived at the tent prior to the service, he noticed an unusual scene. The tent and the entire area around it seemed to be teeming with reporters and photographers, hordes of them, talking to choir members, taking pictures of the giant Bible, speaking to the "regulars"—people who had been attending the services for weeks—and interviewing members of the campaign committee. When the media members saw Billy, they immediately swarmed around him, peppering him with questions, scribbling his answers on their notepads as their flashbulbs went off in his face.

"What's this all about?" Billy asked with a laugh, knowing that up to now, they could hardly have paid reporters to show up at the tent. In fact, other than the paid advertisements run on the church news page of the local papers, the media had ignored the campaign.

"You've been kissed by William Randolph Hearst," one of the reporters quipped.

எல

Born in San Francisco during America's Civil War, William Randolph Hearst grew up in a wealthy mining family. After he was bounced out of Harvard for failing grades and rowdy behavior, he persuaded his father to allow him to take over the *San Francisco Examiner*, which Hearst's father had obtained as payment for a gambling debt owed him. William Randolph Hearst parlayed his family's money into power and influence through a media empire that eventually controlled twenty-eight newspapers and nine magazines, including *Cosmopolitan, Good Housekeeping, National Geographic,* and *Harper's Bazaar.*

Moving to New York, Hearst engaged in a bitter battle with publishing mogul Joseph Pulitzer, owner of the *New York World* daily newspaper. Hearst purchased a competing paper, the *New York Journal,* and proceeded to lure many of Pulitzer's best writers to his stable. He attempted to influence politics in America and elsewhere through the power of the press, printing lurid and often unsubstantiated stories as though true, and sometimes even creating stories out of nothing simply to sell newspapers. Hearst's shady publishing standards, which allowed for sensationalized, scandal-oriented reporting, fostered the term "yellow journalism," ostensibly associated in the public's mind with *The Yellow Kid,* a color cartoon strip in Hearst's *New York Journal.*

Hearst ran for one of New York's seats in the U.S. House of Representatives and won, serving two terms from 1903 to 1907. He ran for mayor of New York City twice, governor of New York once, and even sought the Democratic nomination for president— all without success. Partially to enhance his power in politics, he purchased newspapers in Washington, D.C., Boston, Chicago, Atlanta, Seattle, and Los Angeles.

An avowed hedonist, if not an outright atheist, Hearst struck up a relationship with silent movie actress Marion Davies and carried on a flagrant affair with her throughout his life, although he remained married to Millicent Willson, a former showgirl, with whom he had five sons. Hearst and his wife separated in 1926, and his mistress moved in with him; the couple lived together openly in San Simeon, a magnificent castle Hearst built overlooking the

Pacific coastline. He had the castle ornately decorated—though not always tastefully—with lavish art collections throughout.

Although not specifically stated, the Orson Welles movie *Citizen Kane*, which debuted in 1941, was loosely based on Hearst's flamboyant and highly controversial life. Hearst did all he could to prevent the film from being screened in theaters and banned promotion of the film through his newspapers. The film succeeded, however, and went on to be regarded as one of the best movies Hollywood ever produced, despite Hearst's adamant opposition.

A curious enigma, William Randolph Hearst ran the gamut of philosophical categories. Liberal in his younger years, reactionary as he grew older, some claimed that he supported Adolf Hitler and the Nazis prior to World War II. Originally a leader in the Democratic party, he came to despise Franklin Delano Roosevelt, and he especially opposed Roosevelt's "New Deal," the president's programs intended to put the nation back to work following the Depression. Hearst regarded government-funded employment ventures, such as the Works Progress Administration (WPA) and the mandated Social Security insurance program, as intrusions into the private lives of Americans, setting dangerous precedents for further government control of U.S. citizens. Following the war, Hearst became an isolationist and a staunch anticommunist.

No friend to the gospel, Hearst found evangelists such as Charles Templeton and Billy Graham intriguing nonetheless, and he even invited the two young preachers to spend some time at San Simeon, an invitation that Templeton declined on their behalf. That a man as powerful as William Randolph Hearst—who for more than eight decades had spurned the gospel and lived contemptuous toward its standards of truth and morality—would take an interest in a young preacher holding services in a circus tent is beyond all human explanation.

℗

Billy had never met Mr. Hearst, nor had he ever corresponded with him by phone or letter. He knew that Hearst owned several of the nation's daily newspapers, including the *Los Angeles Examiner*, the city's morning paper, and the *Los Angeles Herald Express*, the evening paper, so he was puzzled by the reporter's caustic comment that he had been "kissed by William Randolph Hearst."

Until the newspapers came out the following day, that is. The headlined stories in Hearst's papers—in Los Angeles as well as New York, Chicago, Detroit, San Francisco, and a wide variety of other cities—all featured Billy Graham and the story of the "Canvas Cathedral" in the middle of the city.

Overnight, the crowds started pouring into the tent for each service. Within days, the tent was overflowing, and the committee added another three thousand seats.

Time magazine ran a feature on Billy, as did the *New York Times*, *Life* magazine, *Newsweek*, and others—all because William Randolph Hearst had ostensibly instructed his editors to "puff Graham." Although Hearst never admitted to the terse command, and his son later denied it, the media did indeed experience a remarkable "conversion" when it came to Billy. Now, everything he said and did was news.

If the press's infatuation with him was an enigma to Billy, it was much more so to his friend, Charles Templeton.

cro

TEMPLETON'S HOSPITAL ROOM, 2001

For the first time since they had begun the interviews, small beads of perspiration formed on Templeton's forehead. But he was so engrossed in the story, Deborah chose not to interrupt or break his train of thought. Templeton seemed in a world of his own anyhow.

"Puff Graham," he snorted. "Make him a star! Ha! Why? Hearst was an atheist. What did he do? Sneak into the revival in disguise? Some people said that happened—that Hearst and his live-in lover, Marion Davies, disguised themselves and attended a meeting in the tent to see for themselves what was going on there." Templeton looked up as though he needed to explain the details more fully to Deborah. "Some people said it was a maid who went down there and told him about it. Maybe so. Nobody knows.

"Two words: *Puff Graham.* That's all old man Hearst said. *Puff Graham.* His reporters knew what that meant: promote Graham; blow him up; write about him; talk about him; make him bigger than life. Amazing, isn't it, how one man's influence could change the course of history? It certainly changed Billy's history, and the history of evangelism." Templeton shook his head slightly, and a worried expression creased his brow. "A bit frightening too, is it not? The way our modern media has the power to build somebody up . . . or tear someone down?" He looked up at Deborah Matthews as though suddenly realizing that she, too, was a reporter.

"Not you, of course," Templeton said with a slightly sardonic laugh. "I'm sure you would never do such a thing."

Deborah shifted uncomfortably in her chair, knowing that she had done precisely that innumerable times in her career. She quickly redirected Templeton's attention back to Hearst and Billy Graham. "But why, Mr. Templeton? Why would William Randolph Hearst do such a thing?"

"I don't know why he did it." Templeton spat out the words. "Hearst cared nothing for Billy Graham, although I suppose in his old age, the newspaper tycoon had grown more conservative, and certainly anticommunist, so he probably enjoyed hearing Billy attack communism as an atheistic religion. But why he would choose Billy over . . . others . . . it defies all logic . . . almost as if Hearst himself was inadvertently playing a role in a much larger production . . . For whatever reason, the word was out: Graham was in.

"And the public responded. Movie stars came down to the tent revival. Gangsters too. The fellow who was the wiretapper for that big gangster, Mickey Cohen. What was his name? Oh yes, Jim Vaus. He was an electronics whiz. But he used his talents for organized crime. He was Cohen's personal wiretapper, but he came down. Walked the aisle in the big tent, like everyone else. Vaus was so excited, he even convinced his boss to invite Billy for a late-night clandestine meeting at Cohen's home. Mickey Cohen wasn't buying what Billy was selling; he was unwilling to give control of his life to Jesus. But thousands of other people did. And Billy's picture was plastered over every newspaper in North America, and *Time* magazine, and *Life* and *Look* as well. And it went on for almost two straight months, from September 25 till Sunday afternoon, November 20. Oh, you should have seen that!" Templeton waved his hand at Deborah.

"Two full hours before the meeting was scheduled to begin, more than eleven thousand people showed up. They packed inside the tent. Thousands more simply milled around outside, but because the public address system was not capable of boosting any more sound, hundreds of other onlookers simply left because they couldn't hear what was going on.

"And by the time Billy and Ruth left Los Angeles and boarded the train back to Minneapolis, he had preached to more than three hundred fifty thousand people. Three hundred fifty thousand! Such a thing had never happened."

"Amazing," Deborah Matthew said, shaking her head. "Tell me something, though. That explains the 1949 event—sort of. But tell me, how did Graham hold mass audiences for more than sixty years, essentially giving the same messages, no new insights, no trendy experiences, yet speaking to hundreds of millions of people. All this, without any 'rock show' gimmicks?"

The cameraman brought the lens in close to Templeton's face. For a moment, Deborah thought the camera may have been a distraction to the old man, and she almost waved the cameraman back. But Templeton didn't even seem to notice. The look in his eyes was on something far-off.

"I can't. I can't," he said softly. Then much more loudly, "I can't!" he said, shaking his head. "And I've asked myself: Why Billy? You would think that if God existed . . ." He paused, surprised at his own vulnerability. But he had gone this far; he might as well go the rest of the way. "You would think that if God existed . . ." He stopped again, his mind struggling to get past those words. "You'd think that if God existed, wouldn't somebody have said, '*Puff Templeton*'?"

Deborah remained quiet for a long few seconds. Looking at Templeton's weary face, for a moment she felt horribly sorry for him. He'd lost so much. His church; his ministry; his reputation; his marriages, first Connie and then Sylvia Murphy, another

attractive woman, who was a Canadian singer, television star, and
sex symbol. He had had children with her, but now she was gone
too. After attending Princeton, he had served as the one and only
national evangelist for the National Council of Churches—an
organization supposedly representing more than thirty-five million
Protestants, including Lutherans, Episcopalians, Presbyterians, and
many Methodists, but by late 1956–early 1957, Charles Templeton
had left the ministry entirely, and everything he associated with
it—including his wife. He had packed up his few belongings in a
trailer and moved back to Toronto. He had then reestablished himself as a television commentator and had even written a few
books—several of which were modestly successful, though none
ever sold in numbers anywhere near Billy Graham's books. Since
then, he had lived in relative comfort and some measure of luxury
with Madeleine, his third wife, until Alzheimer's attacked.

Templeton's question haunted Deborah. Why *hadn't* someone
said, "Puff Templeton"? For all his supposed success, including his
acclaim as an intellectual and an agnostic bright enough to eviscer-
ate most Christians who tried to debate him, Templeton at the
end looked tragically sad. He did not look like a man who had
fought the good fight and won. He did not appear triumphant
and ready to pass on his glorious legacy to the next generation.
What did Deborah see in his eyes as she looked in them again?
Sadness. A deep sense of sadness.

She had to ask him. She knew he may not like it, but she had
one question that for two days had been gnawing at her. She dared
not end their interview without asking. She took a deep breath.

"Mr. Templeton, have you ever considered the possibility . . .
that it was *God*?" she asked quietly.

"What?"

"Well, like you said." Deborah attempted to lighten the mood before coming back at him from another angle. "You can't explain it—yet *it happened.* All that happened to you. And all that happened to Billy—"

"You're aggravating me, young woman," Templeton flared, "and I'm an old man, and I don't need the aggravation." Suddenly his words and emotion poured out like a flood. "Maybe it was God! Maybe it was Jesus! I believe that Jesus was the purest example of all that is good in mankind. I believe that Jesus was the most influential teacher without a doubt in the history of civilization, and I believe that Jesus Christ was the most perfect moral being in the history of the world—"

The old man stopped. It was almost as if his tongue refused to cooperate with what he wanted to say next. As he had done so many times before, in interviews both public and private, Templeton was about to spew his usual punch line: *But he was not the son of God.* That's what he always said. It normally evoked a response everywhere he said it. Christians responded with abject horror and revulsion, not to mention anger so often. Among unbelievers, especially academics, intellectuals, or the pseudointellectuals in Hollywood and Washington, or New York, the remark inevitably elicited rousing agreement and usually cheap rounds of applause. Templeton had said it so many times, with precisely the same inflection that he had used to silence Billy Graham that day so long ago at Forest Home. He just wanted to say it one more time to this reporter and her television crew, but for some reason, the words simply would not come out of his mouth. Instead, he suddenly grew quite emotional. "I believe Jesus was the greatest teacher . . . the most moral person—" He stopped again and looked at Deborah. "And . . . and if you will permit the expression . . . *I miss Him.*"

Tears heavy with remorse dripped from Templeton's eyes as he sobbed quietly. He turned his face away from Deborah, but she could see his shoulders heaving, jerking in spasms. Templeton raised one arm, as though trying to keep the people behind the television camera—the lone operator, the gaffer, and any future viewers—from seeing him.

Deborah Matthews had been around network news for nearly four decades. She had interviewed people from all walks of life, celebrities to no-names. She did not know what to do with this. She sat silently watching the great man weep.

Suddenly Templeton snapped out of it. "Enough of that," he said adamantly. "Enough of this!" He pulled some tissues from a box lying on the table near his bed and wiped his eyes; then he sat up tall and attempted to straighten his robe.

"Mr. Templeton . . ."

"I think it best that you leave now," the elderly man said.

Deborah turned away from Templeton and leaned over to the gaffer who had been drawing the camera cable away from the bed in case Templeton wished them to leave. "Bring him in," she whispered.

She turned back to Templeton. "Yes, sir. You have been more than generous with your time, and it has been a delight talking with you. But before we go, there's somebody who wanted to say hello to you."

"Say hello to me? What? Who?"

"Is he here yet, Frank? I just received a text message that he had arrived at the hospital and was on his way up in the elevator."

"Yes, indeed," the gaffer replied. "He's coming down the hall right now."

The elderly, white-haired gentleman, who had just landed at

the airport a short time ago, moved slowly but resolutely down the hallway toward Charles Templeton's door. In a most unusual request, he had asked his traveling companion to remain in the car for a few minutes. "I want to do this myself," he'd said.

The gaffer came over to Deborah and whispered in her ear. "Okay." She nodded to the cameraman.

"Tape rolling," he said quietly, drawing back unobtrusively.

Deborah turned to Templeton. "He's here."

"Who's here?"

She nodded to the gaffer. "Bring him in."

Deborah turned back to the eighty-three-year-old man in the hospital bed. She hoped he had a strong heart. "Mr. Templeton, there is *someone* who wanted to see you."

"What? Who? Where am I?"

The door to Templeton's room opened, and the elderly gentleman in the black overcoat stepped inside. Templeton's eyes widened in amazement.

"Billy?" he gasped.

Deborah nudged the cameraman. "Do not blow this," she whispered.

"I've got it, Cruella," he responded tersely but quietly.

Eighty-three-year-old Billy Graham crossed the room to Templeton's bed and reached for Chuck's hand, squeezing it gently. "Hello, my dear friend," Billy said in his familiar, clear voice.

Templeton leaned forward and put his head on Billy's shoulder. "It's really you . . . Thank you for coming . . ." Templeton began to weep as Billy held him tightly. "Billy, Billy . . . I have missed you . . ."

"I've missed you as well, Chuck. We've been apart for far too long."

Deborah Matthews felt tears forming in her eyes. She tried desperately to hold them back. She was, after all, a professional. But the tears grew larger and were threatening to fall in large spatters onto her suit. She wanted to blot her eyes with a tissue, but she knew that would only smear her mascara. Too late anyway. The tears were already streaming down her cheeks in tiny rivulets, carving a path through the Pan-Cake makeup coating her face. She didn't even care. Her big story that would supposedly catapult her back to the top of her profession suddenly paled in significance compared to what she was experiencing personally at that moment. She looked at Billy holding his friend with unconditional love, acceptance, and forgiveness, and something deep inside her said, *I want to know that kind of love.*

Templeton looked up, past Billy, and his face appeared puzzled at first, then awestruck, as if he were seeing something astonishing, something marvelously beautiful.

Billy glanced across the bed at Deborah Matthews, who, though ready to ask the two men questions, had backed completely away from them out of respect. Seeing Billy's quizzical expression, she shook her head slightly.

Templeton was smiling—more than smiling. He seemed almost radiant, as he saw what nobody else in the room could see. He turned to Billy and took both of Billy's hands in his. "Billy, Billy . . . you made the right choice."

Billy looked deeply into his friend's eyes. "It's never too late for faith, Chuck. Do you remember the thief on the cross? Everybody else must have thought it was too late for that man. But not Jesus. When the thief called out to Him, Jesus said, 'Today, you will be with Me in paradise.'"

Templeton nodded. "I know, Billy. I know."

Billy spoke tenderly, "It's not too late for you either, Chuck. God loves you and wants you with Him in eternity. You're my friend. You know I wouldn't lie to you—especially now."

"Thank you, Billy," Templeton whispered, as he laid back and closed his eyes.

The nurse motioned for Billy and the others to leave. "He must rest now," she said. "Please, I know you want to stay, but it is time to go."

Billy Graham nodded, and a hint of a smile crossed his face. His work here was done. Billy patted Templeton's shoulder and spoke kindly, "I hope to see you again, Chuck . . . if not here . . ." He paused and pointed toward heaven. "I hope to see you there."

&

Less than six months later, Templeton's wife, Madeleine, was visiting with him in his room, when suddenly he became tremendously excited, his hands waving, his eyes darting to and fro, searching the ceiling, as though seeing something that nobody else could see.

He looked up and smiled, and a peaceful expression washed over his face. "They are so beautiful," he said. "They are waiting for me. Oh, their eyes . . . their eyes are so beautiful . . ."

Templeton blinked to make sure his own eyes were not deceiving him. Then he raised up a few inches off his pillow, opened his eyes wide, and looked heavenward. "I'm coming!" he gasped. "I'm coming."[1]

---

1. Tom Harpur, "Templeton's Widow Tells of 'Transcendent' Deathbed Encounter," *Toronto Star*, June 24, 2001, F3.

Epilogue

The Los Angeles campaign in 1949 launched Billy Graham into international prominence. Scheduled for three weeks, the meetings extended to more than eight weeks, with crowds overflowing the tent erected in downtown L.A. Many of Billy's subsequent early crusades were similarly extended, including one in London that lasted twelve weeks, and a New York City crusade in Madison Square Garden in 1957 that ran nightly for sixteen straight weeks.

After William Randolph Hearst's enigmatic endorsement, "Puff Graham," almost overnight Billy went from being a fledgling evangelist serving with Youth for Christ and as president of a small Midwestern Bible college to the most sought-after speaker in America and abroad. People everywhere wanted Billy and his team to come to their town to help bring spiritual renewal, but as Billy often said, "It was not something we had done. It was God's doing."

Ironically, Billy and Hearst never met; the newspaperman died within two years of the Los Angeles campaign, on August 14, 1951. Nevertheless, Billy Graham went on from Los Angeles to preach the gospel to more people than anyone else in history—speaking to

nearly 215 million people in more than 185 countries and territo-
ries. Hundreds of millions more have been reached through his
television broadcasts, video and audio productions, films, and web-
casts. Since the 1949 Los Angeles crusade vaulted Billy into the
public eye, he has led hundreds of thousands of individuals to make
personal decisions to live for Christ, fulfilling the main thrust of his
evangelistic ministry.

In 1952, Billy resigned as president of Northwestern Schools,
as his divided schedule increasingly caused him to spend more and
more time away from the campus in Minnesota. Although he loved
the board, faculty, and students, he felt that the school would be
better served by having a full-time president. During his tenure,
enrollment at Northwestern had increased from seven hundred
students to twelve hundred, the highest it had ever been. Besides
interacting on a daily basis with young collegians, Billy learned
much from the experience that would be helpful in his future ministry, especially in the areas of finances, logistics, and working with
a wise board of directors whose guidance he had learned to trust.
But relieved of the burden of the school, Billy was able to concen-
trate more fully on what he felt was his first calling—evangelism.

To better conduct their ministry's business, and to avoid any
appearance of the "Elmer Gantry" image of evangelism still held by
many in America, in 1950, Billy and his team—Ruth, T. W. Wilson,
Grady Wilson, and George Wilson, who had helped him at
Northwestern; Cliff Barrows and his wife, Billie, who played piano
for many of the early campaigns; and George Beverly Shea—formed
a nonprofit organization, the Billy Graham Evangelistic Association
(BGEA), initially headquartered in Minneapolis, Minnesota. The
organization relocated to Charlotte, North Carolina, in 2003.

Long before the civil rights movement took hold in America,

in the early 1950s, Billy Graham—a preacher born and raised in South Carolina—challenged the Christian establishment by integrating his crusades. No longer was Billy content to allow black worshipers to be relegated to one portion of the campaign seating while whites were ushered to others. Billy physically stepped down off the platform with dramatic flare and broke the barriers between black and whites, at a significant risk to his ministry. This integration between the races at Billy's events was a major step in American history. Later, Billy developed a strong friendship with Dr. Martin Luther King and helped the civil rights leader bring the concept of a "color blind" society to America. Billy's important influence within the American civil rights movement is an aspect of his ministry that is rarely examined, and often goes without credit from both religious and secular media.

Over the years, Billy and his team grew in influence, Billy becoming a friend and spiritual counselor to every American president from Dwight D. Eisenhower to George W. Bush.

In addition to his numerous evangelistic crusades around the world, Billy and his team expanded their ministry in a wide variety of efforts, including the weekly *Hour of Decision* radio program, broadcast around the world each Sunday for more than fifty years; television specials featuring Billy Graham Crusades and Franklin Graham Festivals broadcast in prime time on an average of 150 stations across the United States and Canada, five to seven times annually; a syndicated newspaper column called "My Answer," carried by newspapers both nationally and internationally; *Decision* magazine, the official publication of the Association, which has a circulation of more than 600,000 and is available in English and German, with special editions available in Braille and on cassette tape for the visually impaired; and World Wide Pictures, which has produced and distributed more than 125 productions, making it one of the foremost producers of evangelistic films in the world. Films have been translated into 38 languages and viewed by more than 250 million people worldwide and are available for showing in correctional facilities nationwide.[1]

During his illustrious career, Billy also produced twenty-seven books, many of which have become best sellers. He was instrumental in the development of *Christianity Today*, a leading magazine among evangelical leaders and laypeople alike. His memoir *Just as I Am*, published in 1997, traces his life from humble beginnings as the son of Frank and Morrow Graham, living on a dairy farm in North Carolina, to the prominence he now enjoys in the hearts of millions of people around the world.

Although Billy once felt intellectually inadequate to lead an academic institution, numerous honorary doctorates from many institutions in the United States and abroad have been bestowed on him. Other highly esteemed recognitions include the Ronald Reagan Presidential Foundation Freedom Award (2000) for contributions to the cause of freedom; the Congressional Gold Medal (1996); the Templeton Foundation Prize for Progress in Religion (1982); and the Big Brother Award for his work on behalf of the welfare of children (1966). In 1964, he received the Speaker of the Year Award and was cited by the George Washington Carver Memorial Institute for his contributions to improve race relations. He was recognized by the Anti-Defamation League of the B'nai B'rith in 1969 and the National Conference of Christians and Jews in 1971 for his efforts to foster a better understanding

---

1. Billy Graham Evangelistic Association Web site: http://www.billy graham.org/MediaRelations_PressReleases.asp.

among all faiths. In December 2001, he was presented with an honorary knighthood, Honorary Knight Commander of the Order of the British Empire (KBE), for his international contribution to civic and religious life over sixty years.

Billy Graham remains popular among everyday people as well; his reputation for integrity is impeccable. In all his years of ministry, not one among Billy's group who signed their "Modesto Manifesto" was ever involved in a financial or moral scandal. Billy is regularly listed by the Gallup polling organization as one of the "Ten Most Admired Men in the World." Gallup described Billy as the dominant figure in that poll since 1948—making an unparalleled fifty-one appearances on that list, forty-four of which have been in consecutive years. He has also appeared on the covers of *Time, Newsweek, Life, U.S. News and World Report, Parade,* and numerous other magazines, and has been the subject of many newspaper and magazine feature articles and books.

Billy and Ruth Graham have three daughters, two sons, nineteen grandchildren, and several great-grandchildren. They lived almost their entire married life in the same home in Montreat, North Carolina.

Perhaps the statement that best summarizes the life of Billy Graham is one he made about himself: "My one purpose in life is to help people find a personal relationship with God, which, I believe, comes through knowing Christ."

Unquestionably, the world is a better place and heaven is more populated because Billy Graham fulfilled that calling on his life.

RUTH BELL GRAHAM

Early in their marriage, with their increased time apart due to frequent preaching trips, Ruth Bell Graham convinced Billy to move the family to Montreat so they could raise their children near her parents. Ruth's ministry flourished in the mountains of western North Carolina, where she built the family homestead and raised the Grahams' five children: Virginia (Gigi), Anne, Ruth (Bunny), Franklin, and Nelson Edman (Ned). Ruth treasured her role as the strong woman behind "America's Pastor" and was Billy's closest confidant, most trusted adviser, and dearest friend. She loved working behind the scenes, away from the spotlight, helping Billy research and craft his sermons and books.

She became known worldwide as a woman of quiet elegance, deep strength, and a great sense of humor. Along with Billy, in 1996, she was awarded the Congressional Gold Medal, the highest civilian award bestowed by the United Stated Congress. The honor was in recognition of their "outstanding and lasting contributions to morality, racial equality, family, philanthropy, and religion."

A gifted poet and writer herself, Ruth authored or coauthored fourteen books, including *Sitting by My Laughing Fire*, *Legacy of a Pack Rat*, *Prodigals and Those Who Love Them*, and *One Wintry Night*. She passed away on June 14, 2007, a few days after she turned eighty-seven.

At her passing, Billy issued a statement: "Ruth was my life partner, and we were called by God as a team. No one else could have borne the load that she carried. She was a vital and integral part of our ministry, and my work through the years would have been impossible without her encouragement and support."

More personally, Billy commented, "I am so grateful to the Lord that He gave me Ruth, and especially for these last few years we've had in the mountains together. We've rekindled the romance of our youth, and my love for her continued to grow deeper every day. I will miss her horribly, and look forward to the day I can join her in heaven."[2]

Ruth was buried at the foot of a cross-shaped walkway and flower garden at the Billy Graham Library in Charlotte, where Ruth and Billy had decided earlier that they would be buried side by side.

CHARLES TEMPLETON

Charles Templeton enrolled in Princeton Theological Seminary in 1948, where he studied for three years, completing all of his academic requirements. He was not, however, awarded a degree since he had not completed high school or his undergraduate studies. During his final year at Princeton, he preached regularly at Ewing Presbyterian Church and was ordained as a minister in the Philadelphia Presbytery, which had specially waived its academic requirements to accept Templeton as a minister. Lafayette College conferred on Charles Templeton an honorary doctor of divinity degree, "in recognition of his contribution to a balanced, intellectually sound and theologically based evangelism."[3]

Following his stint at Princeton, in 1951, Templeton accepted a position with the National Council of Churches as the organization's only evangelist. For a while, Chuck and Connie Templeton lived in Wheaton, Illinois.

He later accepted a position as director of evangelism with the Presbyterian Church USA, in New York City. For nearly

---

2. Jonathan Morris, Fox News, June 15, 2007, *Reactions to Ruth Graham's Death*, http://www.foxnews.com.

3. Templeton, *An Anecdotal Memoir*, 79.

three years, he trained ministers and laypersons, lectured in theological seminaries and universities, wrote two books, and hosted a weekly television program on the CBS network. He continued to preach, mostly as a guest at New York's Fifth Avenue Presbyterian Church.

Connie and Charles divorced, and in the spring of 1957, he left the Christian ministry entirely and moved back to Toronto, where he continued writing, appeared regularly on radio and television, and produced some television programs. He met and married Sylvia Murphy, a popular Canadian singer, with whom he had two children, and adopted two of Sylvia's children from a previous marriage.

He worked briefly as an editor for the *Toronto Star*, and then threw his hat into Canadian politics, running for public office as well as leadership of the Ontario Liberal Party. After a largely unsuccessful and nondescript foray into politics, Templeton returned to writing as an editor for *Maclean's* magazine. He continued his radio show, *Dialogue*, for eighteen years, and additionally worked as a morning newscaster.

Although he and Billy Graham remained friends, Templeton became an avowed agnostic, often speaking antagonistically and condescendingly of Billy's faith. He wrote eight books, including *An Anecdotal Memoir* in 1983, at age sixty-seven. His controversial and much ballyhooed *Farewell to God: My Reasons for Rejecting the Christian Faith* appeared in bookstores in 1995.

When Templeton and his wife, Sylvia, divorced, he married his third wife, Madeleine, with whom he lived in Toronto. He continued to be active, despite the onset of Alzheimer's disease. He worked at inventing toys, succeeding in pitching a heated stuffed animal named TeddyWarm to Mattel, a leading manufacturer of children's toys. In his latter days, Templeton continued to draw, and even used a computer to create new games, exercise equipment, and puzzles to help fight off the effects of Alzheimer's.

He died in June 2001, leaving behind his wife, Madeleine, four children, seven grandchildren, his brother, and a half sister.

T. W. WILSON

Billy's loyal friend T. W. Wilson became an ordained Baptist minister after graduating from college in 1941, and did graduate work at the University of Alabama. He served as Billy's executive assistant, traveling with him worldwide, until he passed away at eighty-two years of age. In addition, he had served as a pastor in Alabama and Georgia and also served as vice president of Youth for Christ. When T. W. passed away, Billy commented, "Ruth and I have lost one of the closest friends we ever had . . . I feel his loss very deeply, but I know where he is. He is in the presence of Jesus, and that's where he longed to be most of his life."[4]

GEORGE BEVERLY SHEA

Singer and radio personality George Beverly Shea also remained a part of Billy Graham's ministry for more than sixty years. He sang each week on Billy's radio program, *Hour of Decision*, and at nearly every crusade Billy conducted. He recorded more than seventy music albums, was nominated for ten Grammy Awards, and won the award for Best Inspirational Performance in 1965. He was inducted into the Gospel Music Hall of Fame, and was often referred to as "America's Beloved Gospel Singer." One of

---

4. "Graham Associate T.W. Wilson, 82, Dies," *Christianity Today*, May 2001, http://www.ctlibrary.com/16498.

his most popular songs was his rendition of "How Great Thou Art."

At ninety-eight years of age, George Beverly Shea sang for the formal dedication of the Billy Graham Library in May 2007 in Charlotte.

CLIFF BARROWS

The personable choir director and emcee for Billy's campaigns, Cliff Barrows continued to work with Billy Graham after their days in Youth for Christ. Along with Billy and George Beverly Shea, he was a part of the original team involved with the 1949 Los Angeles campaign, and he continues to be part of BGEA today. Besides directing the massive choirs at Billy Graham crusades around the world, over the years Cliff Barrows also directed or produced most of Billy's radio and television programs.

GRADY WILSON

Although less visible in public than his brother, T. W., Grady Wilson became a Baptist minister, an effective evangelist, and a close associate of Billy's. The first of Billy's "inner circle" to pass away, Grady died of heart failure when he was sixty-eight. He had been an original member of the BGEA team, and he even filled in preaching for Billy when necessary. Grady Wilson served as vice president of the organization when it was founded in 1950 and remained a trusted advisor to Billy throughout his life.

BOB JONES COLLEGE

Currently known as Bob Jones University
Located at: 1700 Wade Hampton Blvd., Greenville, SC 29609

FLORIDA BIBLE INSTITUTE

Now known as Trinity College in Florida
Located at: 2430 Welbilt Blvd., Trinity, FL 34655; telephone:
800-388-0869

NORTHWESTERN SCHOOLS

Now located at: 3003 Snelling Ave. N., St. Paul, MN 55113;
contact: webmaster@nwc.edu

WHEATON COLLEGE

Wheaton College continues to be recognized as one of the top
Christian liberal arts colleges in the world, maintaining rigorous
academic standards and applying a Christian perspective to all
areas of learning. Former New York Times education editor, Loren
Pope, said, "Wheaton is often called the Harvard of the evangelicals, but that moniker does not do it justice because it is head,
shoulders, and heart above Harvard in its concern with good
moral compasses and strong value systems, as well as in the per-
centage of future Ph.D.s it has turned out."[5]

The Wheaton campus is also home to the Billy Graham
Center, a museum housing many archives relating to Billy's ministry. In addition to Billy and Ruth Graham, other notable
graduates of Wheaton include Donald Soderquist, senior vice
chairman, Wal-Mart; Elizabeth Elliot, author and missionary; J.
Dennis Hastert, former Illinois Congressman and Speaker of the
U.S. House of Representatives; Dan Coats, former U.S. Senator
and U.S. Ambassador to Germany; David Clydsdale, composer;

---

5. Loren Pope, "Colleges That Change Lives," (New York, NY: Penguin,
2000, 2006 editions) (www.ctcl.com).

Gary Chapman, NY Times bestselling author; and Lisa and Todd Beamer, (9/11; United Flight 93).

Located at: 500 College Ave., Wheaton, Il 60187; telephone: 630-752-5909

YOUTH FOR CHRIST

Youth for Christ continues to have a worldwide impact through its work with young men and women. The organization can be contacted at: Youth for Christ, 7670 S. Vaughn Ct., Englewood, CO 80012.

BILLY GRAHAM EVANGELISTIC ASSOCIATION

The ministry of Billy Graham continues through the preaching of his son Franklin Graham, and Franklin's son, Will. The various ministries of BGEA may be contacted through: Billy Graham Evangelistic Association, 1 Billy Graham Pkwy., Charlotte, NC 28201; telephone: 704-401-2432

CPSIA information can be obtained
at www.ICGtesting.com
Printed in the USA
LVOW07s1920170217
524663LV00008B/59/P